Construction techn...
volume 2

J. T. Grundy

BSc, AMICE, MBICSc
Lecturer in construction
Salford College of Technology

Edward Arnold

© J. T. Grundy 1979

First published 1979
by Edward Arnold (Publishers) Ltd
41 Bedford Square, London WC1B 3DQ

Edward Arnold (Australia) Pty Ltd
80 Waverley Road, Caulfield East
Victoria 3145, Australia

Reprinted (with amendments) 1982, 1984, 1986

British Library Cataloguing in Publication Data

Grundy, J T
    Construction technology.
    Vol. 2.
    1. Building
    I. Title
    690   TH145

    ISBN 0–7131–3403–8

Text set in 10/11 pt IBM Press Roman, printed and bound in Great Britain
at The Bath Press, Avon

Contents

Preface

The student should, by now, have seen various forms of construction activity and will have started to appreciate the large variety of methods which may be employed in achieving a given objective. The selection of a particular method will depend upon the site situation and the builder's methods of working.

In this second volume, while adhering to the aims of the level-2 TEC Construction Technology unit, I have endeavoured to provide a broad appreciation of the methods used in the simpler construction procedures.

Acknowledgements

The author wishes to acknowledge once again the assistance that he has received from his wife, friends, and colleagues during the preparation of this volume, particularly from Jack Hodson and Ray Booth.

Copyright material in the form of extracts from the Building Regulations 1985, advisory leaflets, and information and figs 21.3, 21.12, 24.3, and 24.4 relating to sanitation and traffic signs, together with extracts from other government publications, is reproduced by permission of the Controller of Her Majesty's Stationery Office.

Extracts from British Standards are reproduced by permission of the British Standards Institution, 2 Park Street, London W1A 2BS, from whom complete copies can be obtained.

The author would also like to thank the Cement and Concrete Association, Catnic Components Ltd, Key Terrain Ltd, Marley Tile Co. Ltd, IMI Range Ltd, Mercian Site Equipment Ltd, and SGB Group Ltd for their kind assistance with information and diagrams.

J. T. Grundy

1 Site investigations

Understands the need for site investigation and describes typical processes.

1.1 Identifies the information required from a site investigation.
1.2 Describes the purpose of trial pits and hand auger holes.

Acknowledgement is due to the Technician Education Council for permission to use the content of the TEC units in this chapter. The council reserves the right to amend the content of its units at any time.

Once a site has been selected by a developer for a new building project, the suitability of that site for that particular project must be fully investigated. The investigation must be carried out irrespective of whether the site has been previously developed and the buildings are still in existence or have been demolished or the site has never previously been built upon. There are two types of site investigation:

a) that carried out by the client and architect for the purpose of determining the feasibility of the site for its proposed purpose, i.e. where the buildings could be most economically positioned having regard to foundations, topography, services, adjacent buildings, and access.

b) that carried out by the builder or contractor for the purpose of preparing an accurate tender.

A certain amount of the information obtained in (a) will be passed to the builder or made available for his inspection.

1.1 Information required
The following information is required from a site investigation.

a) The topography of the site. This is obtained by carrying out a land survey which, by means of plans and sections, will show the surface features on and adjacent to the site. These features will include the positions of boundaries, trees, hedges, ponds, rock outcrops, roads, footpaths, telegraph poles, gates, buildings on and adjacent to the site, water courses, and ground levels. This information gives the architect an exact record of the surface configuration of the particular site.

b) By reference to ordnance-survey plans and aerial photographs, the situation of the site in relation to a much larger configuration can be seen and assessed, and the possibility of prehistoric remains may also be revealed.

c) Special restrictions on the size of the site may be revealed by inspecting the title deeds of the property. These restrictions may be in the form of (i) covenants relating to noise levels, height of buildings, business restrictions, etc.; (ii) rights of way across the site; and (iii) easements or wayleaves which allow access to overhead or underground services.

d) By reference to geological maps, the main geological formations underlying the site can be seen and assessed for possible problems which may be created as a result of heavy foundation loadings.

e) A visit to the offices of the local planning authority in whose area the site lies will establish (i) the nature of development which will be permitted, (ii) the existence of any planning proposals which may affect the site, and (iii) the existence of any tree or building preservation orders which affect the site.

f) The local highway authority will be able to inform the architect of any road-widening schemes or new road development which may affect the site, together with any restrictions which may be imposed on highway access to and from the site.

g) The service authorities — i.e. water, gas, electricity, post office, and sewers — will be able to indicate on copies of the site survey plan the presence of pipes and cables and their approximate positions. The exact location of these services must be determined by the digging of trial holes, if this information is essential. The authorities will also be able to provide information on the availability of supplies to the site.

h) The water authority or coastguard service can usually provide information on river levels, tides, velocities of tidal and river currents, and areas subject to flooding.

j) The location of mines and shafts under the site may be found from the records of the National Coal Board and other similar bodies, but information relating to mines in operation prior to the First World War is seldom available since these mines were privately owned and few, if any, records were kept. Old local inhabitants or local-history sections of the nearest library are frequently the best sources of information in such cases.

k) Discussion with local residents, especially those having lived in the area for a long time, will produce much useful information about the past history and use of the site; problems attributed to the site in the form of foundation failures, springs, flooding, seasonal swelling and shrinkage of the soil, soil erosion, and earthquakes; and the security of site from vandals or children.

l) Another good indication of the nature of the ground in the area of the site is that of local place or street names, e.g. Springs Estate, Sandy Lane, Coalpit Road.

m) The architect or, in the case of a large project, the structural engineer, is vitally interested in obtaining a soil report on the zone of subsoil likely to affect or be affected by the foundations. The full soil report will show (i) details of the nature and type of strata encountered at various depths at given positions on and possibly around the site, (ii) the level at which ground water was encountered on a particular day(s), (iii) results of laboratory tests on subsoil samples to indicate the likely soil strength, permeability, and elasticity, (iv) the results of chemical analysis of the soil and ground water to determine any possible adverse effects on the foundation structure.

The foregoing information is required by the architect/engineer to assist him in the design of a building so that it will be suitable for its proposed purpose and acceptable to the community at large. In preparing his estimate or tender, it is advisable for the builder or contractor to visit the site itself, armed with the details furnished by the architect in the form of drawings, specifications, and bills of quantities, in order to assess fully the nature and complexity of the proposed works. During that visit he will gather further information which will help in assessing the cost of the work:

n) The state of buildings adjacent to the site, looking especially at their general state of repair and structural condition.
p) The width, state of repair, and materials of the approach and access roads to the site — the movement of heavy excavating machines and construction materials to and from the site may necessitate the construction of new temporary roads or the maintenance, repair, or widening of those roads already in existence.
q) The need for security on the site in respect of (i) theft of goods and materials, (ii) vandalism, (iii) injury to children playing on the site during or after working hours. The results of this investigation will determine whether frequent security-guard visits, a permanent watchman, fencing, hoarding, floodlighting, or a combination of these are required.
r) The local weather conditions. These may have a bearing on how long the work will take and whether special precautions against high winds or heavy rainfall are required during construction.
s) The availability and proximity of tips and their charges for the disposal of surplus excavated material. The cost of long hauls becomes expensive both in fuel and in the number of waggons required.
t) The availability and prices of local building materials such as hardcore, aggregate, ready-mixed concrete, etc. will also significantly affect the cost of the work.
u) The availability of local skilled and unskilled labour will determine whether additional costs are likely to be incurred in transporting labour or, in the case of uninhabited areas, providing labour camps.
v) Where the design team has not carried out a soil survey, the builder may, with the permission of the architect or land owner, carry out his own tests in order to determine for himself the nature of the subsoil conditions.

1.2 Trial holes
The extent of any site investigation will depend on the size and nature of the proposed works, but the cost should be less than 1% of the project costs.

Any investigation of the subsoil will provide the designer with information which will help him in assessing, with some degree of confidence, the behaviour of the natural foundation under load. The information will also assist the builder in assessing the risks and cost of excavation work and will reduce the possibility of claims for additional payment as a result of unforeseen subsoil conditions.

For small buildings having moderate loading conditions – i.e. houses and small factories – the depth of investigation into the subsoil need be no greater than twice the width of the foundation. In the case of a simple house strip foundation, a depth of 2 m to 2.5 m below ground level would be adequate. This depth can be satisfactorily achieved by digging trial pits or boring holes with a hand auger (fig. 1.1).

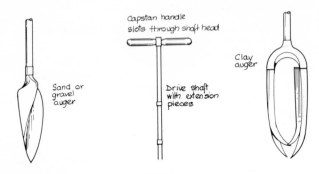

Fig. 1.1 Hand augers

The positioning of these bores or holes on the site will depend on circumstances, but spacings can vary from 15 m to 50 m, either on a grid layout or at random. If the location of the proposed building on the site has been provisionally determined, trial holes or bores should not be excavated on or adjacent to a possible site of foundation construction, since their excavation may cause problems in the construction of the foundations at a later date.

A trial hole is excavated by hand or by mechanical excavator to the required depth, the size being approximately 2 m x 1 m – this allows good visual inspection of the strata and precise location of the water-table level.

The hand-auger borehole does not remove and disturb as much soil as the trial hole, but the nature of the strata can be determined only by inspection of the excavated material brought up by the auger.

Whichever method is used, a precise record of the findings should be kept. The information should include the position of the hole, the method of excavation and the hole size, the date and time of the investigation, the depth of the various strata and a clear description of strata encountered, (see fig. 1.3 for identification), depth at which water was encountered, and the standing water level in the hole. These records are frequently made on some form of standard record sheet (fig. 1.2).

4

BOREHOLE LOG

Site Blue Bell Middleton

Borehole No. 6

B. H. Dia. 0.20 m

Type of Boring Shell & Auger

Ground Level 46.73 m A.O.D.

Date of Boring 25th May 1978

Water Level 1.000 m below G.L.

Remarks Standard penetration tests expressed as 'N' blows per 300 m

Description of Strata	Sample	Depth	B.H.	Depth	O.D.	Remarks
Top soil	D 1	0.15		0.00		
Soft brown sandy clay with fine and medium gravel	D 2	0.30		0.30		
	D 3	0.75 to 1.20		0.60 1.00 1.35		Water encountered — Standing water level
Softish brown and grey sandy clay with fine medium and coarse gravel	D 4	1.50 to 2.00				
	D 5	2.15				
	D 6	3.05				N = 6
Firm brown sandy clay with medium gravel (Boulder clay)	D 7	4.45				N = 7
	D 8	6.00				N = 8
End of Borehole						

D = Disturbed   U = Undisturbed   B = Bulk

Fig. 1.2 Typical borehole record

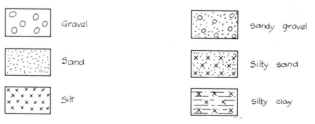

Gravel

Sandy gravel

Sand

Silty sand

Silt

Silty clay

Fig. 1.3(a) Soil identification (*cont'd on page 6*)

5

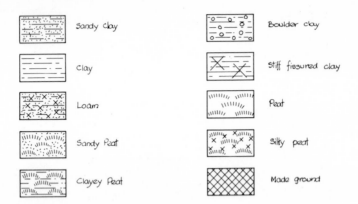

Sandy Clay	Boulder clay
Clay	Stiff fissured clay
Loam	Peat
Sandy Peat	Silty peat
Clayey Peat	Made ground

Fig. 1.3(b) Soil identification (*cont'd*)

2   Site preliminaries

Identifies and describes typical preliminary sitework items.

2.1 *States the implications of protection orders for trees and structures.*
2.2 *Describes means of removing hedges and trees using hand tools and small plant.*
2.3 *Describes typical site security arrangements and explains why these are specific to individual sites.*
2.4 *Describes the procedure for obtaining planning consent for the erection of a site enclosure adjacent to a public highway.*
2.5 *Lists the office accommodation required for a typical site.*
2.6 *States the requirements of the Construction Regulations regarding welfare accommodation on a typical site.*
2.7 *Identifies methods of site storage and degrees of weather protection required.*

Acknowledgement is due to the Technician Education Council for permission to use the content of the TEC units in this chapter. The council reserves the right to amend the content of its units at any time.

2.1 Protection orders

In order to maintain a country's heritage, natural and man-made features of interest or beauty should be preserved. To this end the Town and Country Planning Act of 1971 gave local planning authorities powers to make tree-preservation orders (sections 60–2) and strengthened their powers relating to buildings of architectural and historic interest (sections 54–5) in the interests of amenity.

A tree-preservation order may be made in respect of a single tree, a group of trees, or general woodland which is already in existence or which may be planted conditional on planning consent being given. The effect of the order is to prohibit the cutting down, lopping, topping, uprooting, wilful damage, or destruction of such trees without the prior consent of the planning authority. Even forestry operations may be subject to such an order. Exemptions are made to the order in the case of trees which are dying, dead, have become dangerous, or may be classed as a nuisance under other Acts of Parliament, such trees being cut down in accordance with a felling licence granted by the Forestry Commissioners. Trees having a diameter which does not exceed 75 mm are not affected by an order and those having a diameter not exceeding 100 mm are also exempt provided they are being cut down, uprooted, etc. to improve the growth of other trees. (The diameter is measured over the bark 1.5 m above ground level.)

7

In making a tree-preservation order, the local planning authority must notify the land owners and occupiers of its intentions and also when the order is subsequently confirmed by the Secretary of State for the Environment. If there appears to be 'imminent danger' of a tree being damaged before an order is confirmed, the planning authority may make a special 'provisional' order which is immediately effective and, if unopposed, can be confirmed after 42 days. In the event of opposition to this provisional order, the Secretary of State may confirm the order or it will cease to be effective after six months (or earlier if he rejects it).

The planning authority may require any tree which was subject to an order and has been removed or damaged to be replaced by a tree of similar size and species, in the same place as the original tree.

Confirmation or rejection of an order by the Secretary of State may be challenged on a point of law in the High Courts of Justice.

The penalties for contravening a tree-preservation order are a fine not exceeding £50 and £2 per day for a continuing offence in the case of damage; but, where the tree has been destroyed or is likely to be as a result of lopping or topping, a fine may be imposed of £250 or twice the value of the tree, whichever is the greater.

It is the duty of the local authority to keep available for inspection a register of the trees in its area on which orders have been made.

Listed buildings are those which are on lists compiled by the Secretary of State. They are usually at least 50 years old and are good examples of (a) a particular period of architecture, (b) the work of a particular architect, or (c) buildings or places connected with famous persons and events. It can be seen that the list can contain many diverse items ranging from a mansion to a street lamp, from a pavement to a railway bridge. Local authorities cannot list buildings but can request the Secretary of State to do so. Buildings are listed into grades I, II, or III, grade I being the most important.

The effect of listing a building is to require the owner or occupant to obtain Listed Building Consent before any demolition, alteration, or extension works are carried out, and this requirement can be waived only in the case of a building becoming dangerous. This consent is needed in addition to planning permission, the procedure being that the applicant must advertise his intention on the building or land itself and in the press, there being a 21-day period for objection. If the local authority intends to give consent, it must notify the Secretary of State, who has 21 days in which to confirm or reject the proposals in the case of a grade-I building. If the application is refused by the local authority, the applicant can object and be heard at the resulting inquiry.

There is no obligation on the part of the owner of a listed building to keep it in a good state of repair, but the local authority or the Secretary of State may compulsorily acquire a listed building and adjacent land not kept in reasonable repair. This action must be preceded by the serving of a repairs notice, stating what is required to be done, at least two months beforehand. In a conservation area, the local authority can carry out, in default, repairs of an unoccupied listed building and recover the costs from the owners.

Grants for preserving the external finish or quality of a listed building may be made available by the local authority.

If a listed building is demolished or altered without consent, the local authority or the Secretary of State may issue a Listed Building Enforcement Notice, which specifies the steps to be taken to restore the building to its former state or to such a state as would have been required had consent been given. Failure to comply with this notice in the time specified may result in a maximum fine of £400, and further failure to comply may result in a maximum fine of £50 per day from the date of the first conviction, as well as the local authority entering the site, carrying out the work, and recovering its costs.

The local planning authority may serve a *Building Preservation Notice* on both the owner and the occupier of a building which is not yet listed but is considered to be of special interest and is in danger of demolition or alteration. This notice comes into force immediately it has been served and lasts for six months; its effect is the same as the building being listed. The Secretary of State must confirm or refuse the notice within the six-month period. If the notice is confirmed the building becomes listed; if it is refused the control lapses and the owner or occupier is entitled to compensation for losses incurred as a result of the serving of the notice.

The effect of all these powers is to preserve and conserve the amenities and the environment. In certain cases, they also have the effect of increasing the time to be allowed from the conception of a scheme to the execution of the work, i.e. the precontract period, as well as restricting the architect's design alternatives.

2.2 Clearing the site

One of the first operations on a site is the clearing away of hedges and those trees not affected by preservation orders. The method of removal will depend on their size and the equipment available to the contractor.

The methods available are

a) *Pushing out* by means of a bulldozer. This may be done provided the root system is neither deeply embedded nor extensively spread in the ground.

b) *Digging out* by means of a mechanical excavator, using a backactor or front bucket, or hand excavation using pick and spade. In the case of hand excavation it may be better to cut through the majority of the roots and leave the remainder either to decay in the ground or to be excavated at a later date during reduced-level or trench-excavation work.

c) *Pulling out* by means of a chain or wire wrapped around the tree and attached to a dozer, tractor, lorry, or winch. There is seldom any indication of the force being exerted on the chain or wire during this method of removal and injury to equipment and personnel may result if a fracture occurs, especially when using a wire, where there is a whiplash action. Tracked or wheeled plant will require good ground traction, while mechanical or hand winches will require a good anchorage for the winch, sometimes provided by other trees in the vicinity.

9

d) *Burning down*   Small hedges and shrubs may be burnt down, provided suitable precautions are taken to restrict flame spread.
e) *Cutting down*   Trees or hedges may be cut down either partially or fully. Partial cutting, i.e. the removal of the branches and tops, will restrict damage done to surrounding trees and buildings when final removal is carried out by one of the other methods, including full cutting down or felling. Cutting down may be carried out by axe, hand saw, or mechanical saw. The level at which felling is carried out on a tree is usually 0.6 m to 1 m above ground level — this leaves the stump and root system to be dealt with in other ways.
f) *Destruction*   There are occasions when there is a time lag between the felling of trees and the start of construction work, and in such cases a hole be bored down into the stump of the trees and chemicals such as creosote may be poured in. These have the long-term effect of destroying the stump and roots. Very large tree stumps can be removed by the use of small explosive charges.

2.3 Site security

Site security is an important factor in any construction operation, and certain aspects of this have been previously mentioned in section 1.1 (q). There are three main aspects to be considered:
a) *Loss of goods and materials*   It is difficult to quantify the cost of these losses as distinct from material misuse and wastage, but estimates as high as 5% of total material costs have been made, materials being taken from the site by those working there and by outsiders gaining access.

Small valuable items or those items which are of use to householders or tradesmen rather than having resale or scrap value, e.g. plumbing and electrical fittings, can be stored in locked cabins which have either no windows or a facility for boarding up the windows at the end of each working day. On a large site, storemen may be employed specially to deal with the receiving and issue of such goods.

Larger or more bulky items are more difficult to secure, and to protect these a deterrent such as fencing or hoardings is used. For items such as kitchen or cupboard units a large enclosed storage area is required, not only for security but also to prevent the units from physical or climatic damage. A storehouse which may be easily erected on site for the duration of the work or a convenient building close to the site is frequently used. If the site is already secured by a fence and deliveries of the units are suitably phased, new buildings which have already been erected and which are weather-tight can be secured by glazing and external lockable doors to provide suitable storage accommodation.

Items of timber such as floor joists are generally not susceptible to pilferage, but floorboarding can be put to many uses and should be stored out of sight of the passer-by. Theft of bricks, sand, course aggregate, etc. is seldom a problem, but losses resulting from spread of these materials due to incorrect storage may be high.

On large construction sites with a big administrative section, office equipment, money, and records must be secured. Again the degree of security appropriate to the risk must be considered, but safes, alarm systems, night watchmen, and security patrols are all possible solutions.

b) *Vandalism*   This is usually perpetrated by outsiders rather than by employees, so the exclusion of outsiders from the site is of prime importance. Breaking of glazing in new and unoccupied buildings is a problem, and if it is possible to erect hoardings they may well prove to be economic in a vandal-prone area. The prosecution of those caught causing damage may also indirectly improve site security.

c) *Injury to children*   However many notices are erected and however often children are told not to play on a building site, the temptation to do so is irresistible. There are places to hide, things to climb, sand to play in, machines to drive, and pipes to crawl through. Danger is present in every one of those activities, day or night, and even an eleven-year-old child does not fully appreciate that fact — nor in law is it expected to. The builder must, therefore, provide some barrier which can reasonably be expected to prevent the entry of children. Alternatively, if there are only a few children in the neighbourhood, a watchman or security patrol might be sufficient.

Security is also required where the site is in a congested city-centre area and deep excavation is being carried out close to pavements. In this instance the general public must be kept away for its own good — there is nothing more interesting than watching, at close hand, someone else working.

Further instances of security requirements are those of top-secret government projects such as headquarters for the armed forces, police headquarters, nuclear power stations, and armament factories.

It can be seen from the above that the security of each site must be considered on its merits and individual solutions devised. The most common solutions are fencing and hoarding (fig. 2.1).

Chain-link fencing is supported at intervals of approximately 3 m by intermediate posts, and the whole fence is kept taut by two, three, or four strands of straining wire anchored to straining posts every 25 m. The posts may be concrete or steel and should be let at least 700 mm into the ground and surrounded with concrete. Additional security may be provided by height (up to 3 m) and by sloping anti-intruder arms fixed to post tops and carrying lines of barbed wire.

Hoardings are usually constructed from plywood sheets (2.4 m x 1.2 m) which may be new or may have previously been used for formwork. They are supported on timber posts 100 mm x 50 mm or 75 mm at 1.2 m centres. Provision of holes or vantage points may be considered a good public-relations exercise, especially on prestigious contracts.

2.4 Planning permission for site enclosures

Where a site enclosure is to be erected adjacent to a highway, the first consideration must be not to restrict or divert the vision of vehicle drivers. It is

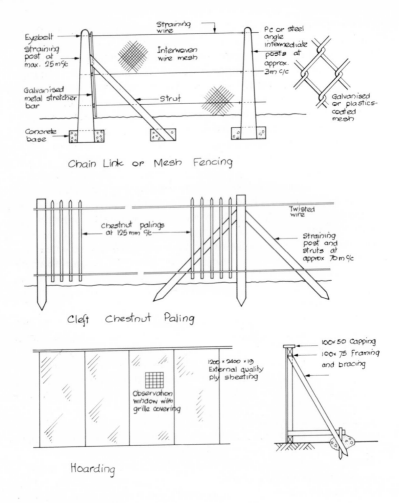

Fig. 2.1 Site enclosures

good practice to consult with the local-authority highway section before any proposals are finalised.

The consideration of restricted vision is especially important at road junctions, where, rather than the erection of hoardings, chain-link fencing may provide the clear vision needed for safety. At city-centre sites, hoardings provide safety for pedestrians but give a free advertising board for bill-stickers — the posters possibly distracting a driver's attention from the highway.

In general, there is no requirement for planning permission for the erection of temporary works, e.g. fences and cabins, in connection with an approved development, unless fences are

a) over 1m high adjacent to a highway,
b) over 2 m high on the site itself
and in both cases the enclosure remains erected for more than 28 days. The same criteria apply in the case of floodlights over 2 m above the ground.

Planning-application forms are available from the local authority, who may or may not require drawings of the proposals. The approval for the erection of the enclosure, as with other planning applications, may be conditional on such factors as the colour of paint to be used on the hoarding or a ban on bill-posting.

2.5 Site offices
Office accommodation provided on a site varies from one contractor to another and depends on the size and value of the contract, the distance of the site from the contractor's head office, and the contractor's site-management policy.

On a typical contract of between £1m and £2m in value, the office accommodation provided should allow for the personnel listed in fig. 2.2 (typical floor areas are given in parentheses).

Contractor:
a) Site agent/site manager/contract manager (11 m^2)
b) Site engineer(s) (9 m^2)
c) General foreman (9 m^2)
d) Trades foremen (11 m^2)
e) Bonus surveyors (9 m^2)
f) Quantity surveyors (12 m^2)
g) Time-keeper/wages clerk (8 m^2)
h) Storeman/checker (6 m^2)
j) Typist clerk (8 m^2)

Client:
k) Resident engineer (10 m^2)
l) Clerk(s) of works (12 m^2)
m) Quantity surveyors (10 m^2)

n) Conference area (20 m^2)

Fig. 2.2 Typical office requirements for site staff

It should be noted that the job titles and specifications mentioned above will vary from area to area and employer to employer, and the areas given may well be combined (and reduced) to suit the particular site organisation. Small sites may have only one or two offices, since the foreman may fulfil many of the site functions, while larger sites, especially those in isolated areas, may include personnel offices and a much larger administrative section (fig. 2.3).

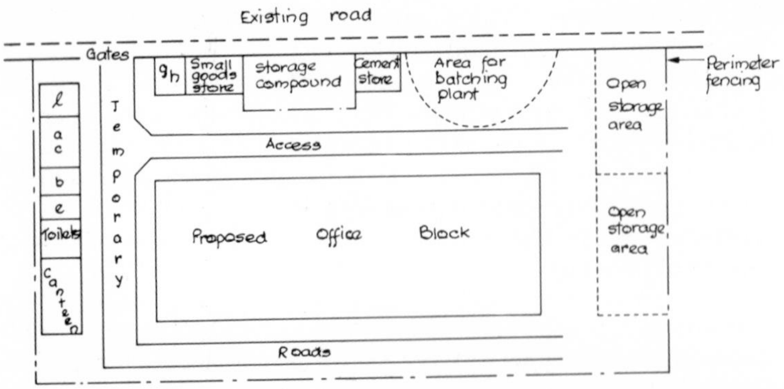

Fig. 2.3 Typical layout of site accommodation (N.B. Office lettering refers to accommodation shown in fig. 2.2)

2.6 Welfare accommodation

The general site-accommodation requirements for the labour force are covered by the Construction (Health and Welfare) Regulations 1966, made under the Factories Act of 1961, which apply both to building operations and to works of engineering construction. The requirements of the regulations vary according to the number of people employed on the site.

Shelter is required for the men during bad weather, and somewhere to deposit the clothes not worn during working hours. Where more than five men are employed, there must be facilities for them to warm themselves and dry out their wet clothes. There should also be facilities for the storage and drying of protective clothing. The shelter provided on site will usually double as accommodation for eating meals, with sufficient seats and tables being provided as well as facilities for boiling water — no workman can go without his 'cuppa'! Drinking water should also be provided at convenient points.

Where there are more than ten men employed, additional facilities are required for heating food, unless a canteen is provided. The regulations also require these shelter and messing facilities to be kept clean and orderly and not to be used for storing materials and plant. Therefore, depending on the size of the site, labour may be employed full-time or part-time on welfare duties.

The provision of sanitary facilities is also a requirement of these regulations.

a) *Sanitary conveniences*   One water or chemical closet must be provided for every 25 employees on a site with up to 100 employees and, providing that sufficient urinals are provided, one for every additional 35 employees on sites with more than 100 employees; e.g. for 185 employees, seven closets and four urinals would be required. These conveniences should be (i) adequately ventilated, (ii) under cover, (iii) suitably partitioned and having doors with fastenings, and (iv) should not communicate directly with workrooms or messrooms.

14

b) *Washing facilities*   These must be provided if any person is to be on the site for more than four hours. Where more than 20 people are employed and work is unlikely to be completed in less than six weeks, adequate troughs, basins, or suitable buckets must be provided, together with hot and cold water, soap, and towels. Where there are more than 100 employees on the site and the works will take longer than 12 months, 'adequate' is deemed to be four wash-basins plus one for every additional 35 employees in excess of 100; i.e. the same number of wash-basins are required as toilets.

On large sites, i.e. those which employ more than 250 people, in addition to the messing and sanitary accommodation, a contractor who employs more than 40 people must provide a first-aid room containing a sink with hot and cold water, a smooth impervious-topped table, a couch, a foot-bath, stretchers, blankets, a means of sterilising equipment, and bandages — the room having interior surfaces capable of being easily kept clean.

The regulations also require the provision of a first-aid box on smaller sites and lay down the minimum contents of such boxes.

2.7 Storage accommodation

The building site is a place for putting together many different materials and components. If work is to proceed smoothly, those materials and components should be to hand as and when they are required, and ideally this means that the materials should be delivered no sooner than the day before they are required. However, in practice this is seldom possible, even with much advance planning and updating of work programmes. It is therefore necessary to obtain materials — some of which may be in short supply — well in advance of site requirements, thereby incurring problems of storage.

The cost of storing materials and components can be divided into two: (a) the cost of providing accommodation, (b) the cost of additional handling. Both these costs reduce the profit margin of a contractor and must be kept to a minimum.

Storage accommodation is provided for two main reasons, namely the prevention of damage and the security aspects which were discussed earlier in the chapter. Damage may be caused either by the weather or by physical agents, and the degree of protection is therefore geared to these factors.

It has been previously stated that lock-up cabins or secured site buildings provide good security; they also give good weather protection. However, the amount of weather protection required varies from material to material. Methods of storage may be listed as follows:

1. site hut with windows and lockable door,
2. plain cabin or shed with lock,
3. house shell — unsecured,
4. covered racks,
5. uncovered racks,
6. bunkers or bins,

Material/component	Degree of protection	Storage method	Notes
Aggregates	(iv)	6, 7	Excessive moisture or frost may restrict laying.
Bricks	(iv)	7	Rapid deterioration on contact with moisture.
Cement	(i)	1, 2, 8	
Drainage goods – earthenware	None	7	Prevent physical damage.
plastics	(iv)	5	
pitch fibre	None	7	
cast iron	None	7	
Glass-fibre quilt	(iii)	2, 3	Partial protection provided by packaging.
Joinery – doors	(i)	1, 2	Internal doors warp and twist with change in moisture content.
flooring	(i) and (ii)	2, 3	Kiln-seasoned material must be kept at a constant moisture content.
stairs	(ii)	3, 4	
units	(ii)	1, 2	
Plumbing fittings and units	None	2	Security important.
Roofing felt	(iii)	2	Security important.
Roof tiles	None	7	
Small plant	(iii)	2, 8	Electrical goods need both protection and security.
Steelwork	None	2, 8	Security of small items.
Timber – boards	(ii)	1, 2, 3	
external	None	5, 7	
structural	(iv) and (v)	5, 7	
studding	(iii)	4	
windows	None	5, 7	

Fig. 2.4 Materials and their protection

7. stockpiles with or without covers,
8. special storage — e.g. silo, garage, oil tank.

On a well organised site on which the materials have been correctly stored, damage by physical means is seldom a problem. The degree of weather protection should be commensurate with the risk, e.g. no damage will be done to rain-water pipes if they get wet, but costly damage will be incurred if cement is allowed to get wet.

There are several degrees of protection, which can be classified as follows.
  i) Total — material to be protected at all times from weather and its effects; moisture content critical.
 ii) Good — material to be protected from weather; moisture content important.
iii) Partial — keeps rain off, but material open to atmosphere.
 iv) Intermittent — protection required only at certain times or damage may be caused as a result of weather action, e.g. frost or mud.
  v) None — no damage will be incurred by exposure to the weather.

The table in fig. 2.4 gives the degree of protection required and the method of providing that protection for a selection of materials and components.

Site accommodation is available in many forms (fig. 2.5), and these may be classified as
a) portable,
b) sectional,
c) framed,
d) semi-mobile,
e) mobile,
f) air-house.

a) *Portable*   These are small lightweight units manufactured in aluminium, glass fibre, or plastics. They will accommodate a small number of workmen and can be easily lifted on and off the back of a waggon by hand. Toilet accommodation is also available in this form.
b) *Sectional*   Generally constructed of timber, these units are the most popular because the sections forming floors, walls with windows, walls with doors, blank walls, and roofs can be erected by use of bolts or nails in any configuration to suit site requirements and are easily dismantled on completion. The internal division of the accommodation is achieved by using fibreboard sheets fixed to a timber framework. These sections are easy both to store and to maintain. This form of accommodation is suitable for offices, messrooms, toilets, and stores.
c) *Framed*   Generally the frame of this type of accommodation is formed of steelwork, with the cladding being of galvanised steel, asbestos cement, aluminium, or brickwork. A certain amount of foundation work is required for these structures, but on a large site the availability of a large storage area may be worth the additional expense.

17

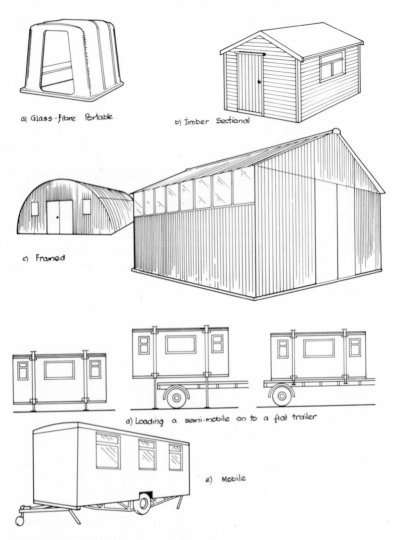

a) Glass-Fibre Portable

b) Timber Sectional

c) Framed

d) Loading a semi-mobile on to a flat trailer

e) Mobile

Fig. 2.5 Types of site accommodation

d) *Semi-mobile*   These are prefabricated units which may be purchased completely fitted out with furniture, wiring, and plumbing as required, the services being ready for connection on arrival on site. They consist of a steel framework clad with plywood, chipboard, hardboard, or plastics, having an attractive weather-resistant exterior finish and a suitable interior finish. The framework is rigidly attached to four legs, which accommodate a jacking mechanism, or to lifting points. The cabins can be jacked up to such a height that a flat-topped waggon can drive under-

18

neath and transport the whole unit away; alternatively, they may be lifted by crane on to the transport vehicle. These cabins are ideal for setting up on undulating ground, but are not generally suitable for use as storage accommodation. By virtue of the strength of the legs, which extend to the full height of the unit, it is possible to stack one unit on top of another — this is ideal for sites where there is limited space for accommodation.

e) *Mobile*   Similar units to those described in (d) are available on wheels (e.g. caravans), but their length must be restricted for towing purposes.

f) *Air-house*   This an inflatable p.v.c.-coated nylon-fabric envelope attached around its base perimeter to the ground. Various shapes and sizes are available, and the structure is ideal for storage accommodation as well as providing enclosed winter-working conditions. The only drawback is that of time loss due to passing through the air lock.

3   Identification of services

Understands the principles of locating, identifying and protecting public utility services.

3.1   Lists the public utility and other services which may be encountered.
3.2   Lists the Authorities responsible for these services.
3.3   Identifies the need to notify these Authorities regarding location, protection, alteration or termination.
3.4   States recommended methods of identifying and marking existing services.

Acknowledgement is due to the Technician Education Council for permission to use the content of the TEC units in this chapter. The council reserves the right to amend the content of its units at any time.

3.1 Utilities
The services which may be encountered on or around a site are
a) water,
b) gas,
c) electricity,
d) telephone,
e) sewerage,
f) oil,
g) district heating,
h) television.

3.2 Responsible authorities
The major services have already been discussed in Volume 1 (section 15.1). All the services listed above can be classified into three distinct areas of responsibility: national, regional, and local.

a) National
  i) *Gas*   The British Gas Corporation is required to develop and maintain a system of gas supply for the country.
  ii) *Electricity*   The Central Electricity Generating Board is responsible for the generation and primary distribution of electricity through the national grid.
 iii) *Telephone*   British Telecom has under its direction all aspects of telecommunications.
 iv) *Oil*   The British National Oil Corporation has powers to operate pipelines in connection with petroleum.

b) Regional

i) *Water and sewerage*   Great Britain is split up into autonomous regional authorities who have overall responsibility not only for water supply and sewerage but also for river and coastal works.

ii) *Gas*   There are a number of regional boards who are responsible for the distribution of gas within their own area.

iii) *Electricity*   There are fourteen regional boards whose responsibility is for secondary and local distribution of electricity within their own areas.

iv) *Telephone*   There are eleven regions which administer the telecommunications system.

c) Local

i) *Water and sewerage*   For administrative convenience, the regional authorities are split into a number of smaller areas and sections so that specialist or local knowledge, information, or action can be more readily available to the general public.

ii) *Gas*   The regional boards are subdivided into smaller more manageable areas in a similar manner to the water authorities, but also maintain customer liaison by means of town-centre showrooms.

iii) *Electricity*   The regional boards have a similar subdivision system to those of the gas boards, although the area boundaries are not the same.

iv) *Telephone*   The regions are subdivided into sixty-two areas, each having an administrative office responsible for the running of the area system.

v) *District heating*   This is generally under the direction of the local authority, whose own properties and estates are supplied with heat from a central boiler-house in the neighbourhood.

vi) *Television*   In certain areas, the erection of television aerials on the roofs of properties may be forbidden by planning officers. In such cases properties will be supplied with a signal by means of underground cables and boosters from one conveniently located aerial. The operation of such a system is generally in the hands of a local or national commercial interest.

3.3 Notification

It has already been indicated in section 1.1 that the site investigation, when carried out fully, should reveal the presence of the various services.

a) *Location of services*   The scale of a site plan is too small to indicate the exact location of a given service. In returning plans suitably marked to indicate the location of a given service, the service authorities usually include a statement that the position is only approximate and care should be taken when work is begun in the area.

b) *Protection of services*   Services are protected in a number of ways (see Volume 1, section 15.4), but the power and reach of modern excavating machines, together with their bucket capacities, can make a nonsense of such protection. Therefore, when any excavation work is to be carried out in the vicinity of known services, notices should be served on the particular service authority or owner. Many of the authorities employ and retain men whose local knowledge of their respective services is invaluable and whose presence on site at the start of work may save all parties both time and money. This presence is readily available when requested. However, many instances occur when, even after the most careful investigation, enquiries, and tests, service lines are fractured. These fractures may result in a loss of supply to industries where the continuity of supply is vital, with consequent loss of production, or damage and danger. For this reason, certain authorities can obtain an indemnity against damage of their buried services or can require special precautions to be taken during the excavation works.

c) *Alteration to services*   Generally, alteration works are carried out by the particular service authority or its subcontractor, and the cost of the works is charged to the developer. These costs may be reduced in part or in full if as a result of the alteration the authority gains advantage (from sales or revenue).

d) *Termination of supply*   Notice of termination of the requirement of a supply must be given to the various authorities so that they may carry out such work as they deem necessary to protect their pipes and installations or to render them harmless to the general public — this is especially important in demolition and development areas.

Pipe contents	*Basic identification colour*
Water	Green
Steam	Silver-grey
Oils (mineral, animal, vegetable, combustible liquids)	Brown
Gases (except air) in gaseous or liquefied condition	Yellow ochre
Acids and alkalis	Violet
Air	Light blue
Other liquids	Black
Electrical services and ventilation ducts	Orange

Other codes include colours for safety, such as	
Red	Fire-fighting
Yellow with black stripes	Warning of danger
Yellow with black trefoil	Ionising radiation

Fig. 3.1 Table of basic colours for pipe identification.

3.4 Identification of services

The identification of services is of prime importance, especially inside a building where several services are contained within the same service ducting.

Pipelines are identified by a basic colour, fig. 3.1.

The basic colour identification of services is detailed in BS 1710: 1984, the colour being applied over the whole length of the pipe or as a band over a length of 150 mm, depending on the pipe diameter.

A further colour code over and above that indicated in fig. 3.1 is used for safety purposes or where a more precise knowledge of the contents of a pipeline is required. In this case, basic colour identification is applied in two 150 mm-wide bands with a 100 mm-wide safety or identification colour between them (fig. 3.2).

It should be noted that the means of identification should be placed at all junctions, at both sides of valves, bulkheads, and wall penetrations, and at other places where identification may be necessary.

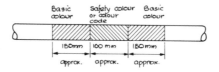

Pipe contents	Basic colour	Colour code
Water:		
drinking	Green	Auxiliary blue
cooling (primary)	Green	White
boiler feed	Green	Crimson—white—crimson
central htg <100 °C	Green	Blue—crimson—blue
central htg >100 °C	Green	Crimson—blue—crimson
cold down service	Green	White—blue—white
hot-water supply	Green	White—crimson—white
fire extinguishing	Green	Safety red
Compressed air		Light blue
Vacuum	Light blue	White
Steam		Silver-grey
Drainage		Black
Oils:		
diesel fuel	Brown	White
furnace fuel		Brown
lubricating	Brown	Emerald green
hydraulic power	Brown	Salmon pink

Fig. 3.2 Diagram and table of pipework colouring code

4 Excavation

Describes the process of excavating up to 2.500 m deep.

4.1 Describes processes for:
  a) site clearance and stripping of topsoil.
  b) excavating to reduced levels.
  c) excavating trenches and pits.
4.2 Describes the effects of soil type and ground-water table on excavation procedure.
4.3 States the primary factors concerned with temporary support of excavations to ensure a safe working environment.
4.4 Sketches and describes open timbering and vertical close timbering.
4.5 Describes the use of small pumps for the removal of water from excavations.

Acknowledgement is due to the Technician Education Council for permission to use the content of the TEC units in this chapter. The council reserves the right to amend the content of its units at any time.

4.1 Site preparation

a) Site clearance

This not only involves the removal of trees, shrubs, hedges, etc., as described in Chapter 2, but may also include the demolition of existing structures on the site.

Demolition is a specialist operation and should not be attempted by the builder on anything but the smallest outbuildings. By employing a reputable demolition contractor, there are many advantages to be gained: he can salvage the material and will have ready outlets for it, thereby reducing the cost of the operation; he can appreciate the factors affecting safety; and he will also have adequate insurance cover in the event of any mishaps.

Safety is the all-important factor and applies not only to the work-force but also to the general public, adjoining property, and services.

There are two types of demolition: total and partial. Total, as the name implies, is where the whole structure is demolished. Partial is where only part of the whole structure is removed, either internally as for alteration works, externally as for a face-lift, or a combination of the two as, for example, in the case of replacing an existing wing of a hospital with a new one.

The methods of demolition depend upon the type, size, state, and position of the building in question.

i) *Hand*, using sledge-hammers, chisels, picks, and crowbars   Generally the
   sequence of operations is the reverse of the structural erection procedures.
   This method is suitable for confined sites, internal work, or where there
   is valuable material to be reclaimed, e.g. lead, roof slates, timber, etc.
ii) *Fragmentation*   As the name implies, this is the process of reducing the
   building to a heap of rubble by the cheapest method. The methods available are

   explosives — requiring the services of a person qualified to handle them.
   cast-iron or concrete ball — the ball is substituted for the bucket on a
                                drag-line excavator and is swung against or
                                dropped on the building.
   wire hawser — attached to a bulldozer or tractor and wrapped around a
                 section of the building, the hawser slices through the
                 structure or pulls it over.
   timber baulk — inserted into a special cup on the bucket of a front-loader
                  excavator, the free end is positioned against a section of
                  the building and, using the tractive force of the machine,
                  pushes that section over.
   Other ancillary equipment used in the demolition process includes
pneumatic drills, oxy—acetylene burners, thermic lances, and lasers.

b) Excavating to a reduced level

The reasons for the removal of the top soil and the methods available have
been fully covered in Volume 1 (Chapter 5).

For excavation to a reduced level, it is necessary to establish that level on
site. This is achieved by means of sight rails and boning rods.

Horizontal rails are fixed to pegs around the proposed excavation, each
rail being at the same level above a given datum. These sight rails should be
set at such a height above ground as to be convenient for sighting over. The
difference in level between the site rails and the reduced level can be calculated. A wooden staff with a cross-piece forming a tee is cut to the
calculated length (the boning rod), and, without resort to further levelling
work, the reduced level can be established by sighting the top of the boning
rod between two or more sight rails (fig. 4.1).

The method of excavating will depend upon the plant available, but the
excavation will usually have sloping sides unless the work is being carried
out on a confined site. The process consists of the machine excavating to
the full depth required, a section at a time, and depositing the excavated
material into a waggon, parked alongside, which will remove the material
to the tip. The waggon should be parked in such a position as not to inter-
fere with the digging cycle of the machine, but at the same time reducing
the slewing of the machine to a minimum and also remaining on stable
ground itself. The number of waggons required should take account of the
output of the excavator, the time taken for a round trip to the tip by each
waggon, and the carrying capacity of the waggons involved.

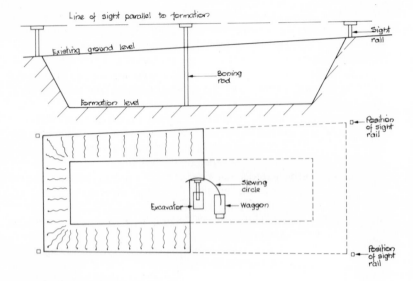

Fig. 4.1 Reduced-level excavation

c) Trench excavation

The amount of excavation required on site for trenches and pits is again determined by means of sight rails and boning rods. The positions of the trenches for the strip foundations of a building are established by means of profiles. Having established the positions of the corners of the building, the profiles (horizontal boards nailed to two stout posts driven into the ground) are set up clear of the trenches, so as not to obstruct the excavation work (fig. 4.2). The positions of the trench and walls are marked on the top of the board by nails or saw cuts, so that lines can be strung from profile to profile indicating the exact run and width of trench or wall. If the tops of all the profile boards are kept at the same level, then the profile can also be used as a sight rail (fig. 4.3).

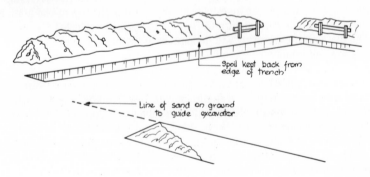

Fig. 4.2 Trench excavation

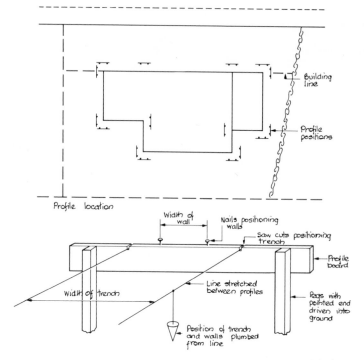

Profile location

Width of wall

Nails positioning walls

Saw cuts positioning trench

Profile board

Width of trench

Line stretched between profiles

Pegs with pointed end driven into ground

Position of trench and walls plumbed from line

Building line

Profile positions

Fig. 4.3 Profiles

Foundation-trench excavation is usually carried out by means of a back-actor excavator or by hand. As most of the excavated material will be used to backfill the trench on completion of the substructure works, it is deposited alongside the trench, but not so close to the edge as to cause that edge to give way under the additional loading. The mechanical equipment will excavate to the full depth at one pass, whereas with hand excavation several passes will be required, especially in excavations exceeding 1.5 m deep, where the labourer will be unable to 'throw out' the excavated material with ease.

4.2 Soils
The nature of the soil will determine the ease with which it may be excavated; generally, the higher the bearing capacity of the subsoil, the harder it will be to dig through. However, cohesive properties are an additional factor. Loose-grained materials such as gravel, sand, and silt will tend to fall away to their natural angle of repose (the angle which the sides of a heap of material will make with the horizontal when tipped, fig. 4.4). Unless some form of side support is provided, this will result in over-excavation, especially in trenches where the sides are generally required to be vertical.

27

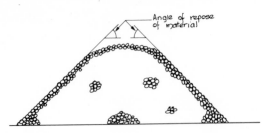

Fig. 4.4 Angle of repose

The level of the water table is also of concern since, if an excavation is required to be taken down below that level, the water present will hamper the operation: it can obscure the excavator driver's view of the bucket; wash some of the excavated material out of the bucket, thereby reducing the output of the machine; erode the sides of the trench, causing collapse with resulting delays; and cause problems in bottoming the trench to receive the artificial foundation. The presence of water in subsoil exposed by excavation may cause particular strata to collapse, since moisture content will affect the angle of repose of certain soils. The presence of water will also cause difficulties in hand excavation, since an increase in the moisture content of a soil will give an increase in mass per unit volume over that of the dry soil.

It is therefore essential to a contractor that he has prior knowledge — in the form of trial holes and test reports — of the ground conditions he is likely to encounter, so that he can both estimate the cost and plan the sequence of the excavation works with reasonable accuracy. The cost increases not only as a result of slower excavation rates but also through having to use heavier or more powerful equipment and, in the case of ground water, the cost of removing it from the excavation by pumps or other means, or preventing its entry into the trench in the first place.

4.3 Temporary ground support

Certain types of ground will maintain a vertical face without support when a trench is excavated; other types will require varying degrees of support. It is, however, good practice to provide some form of support to the sides of all trenches, since what may appear to be 'good' ground could be hiding 'bad' ground immediately behind it.

The main factors to be considered in determining if temporary support is to be provided to the sides of an excavation are

a) The safety of the men working in the trench. The workman is at risk from (i) the sides of the trench collapsing, (ii) soil falling from the sides of the excavation, (iii) material falling into the trench from above, (iv) other men falling into the trench, (v) the excavating machinery in operation, and (vi) vehicles being driven into the excavation.

b) The safety of surrounding property and roads. Any collapse or ground movement may affect the foundations of the surrounding property, causing settlement.

c) Allowing the construction work to proceed in an orderly manner without undue haste, since such haste may result in safe working conditions being ignored.

The type and amount of support provided should depend upon

d) The nature of the subsoil. Soil may collapse as a result of
   i) simple mechanical failure — the inability to support its own weight;
   ii) breakdown of the strength by moisture — caused by a high water table, heavy rain, or frost;
   iii) vibration from the movement of vehicles nearby;
   iv) heavy loads placed near the edge of the excavation;
   v) the excavation being in close proximity to the site of a previous excavation;
   vi) variations in soil type, e.g. pockets of sand;
   vii) heavy objects striking the sides of the trench, e.g. large drain-pipes.
e) The length of time the trench will remain open before backfill.
f) The depth of the trench.
g) The work to be carried out. Large-diameter drainage pipes will require a clear run at the bottom of the trench.
h) The prevailing weather conditions.
j) The method of excavation — a machine bucket will not be affected by a trench collapse, whereas a man might be killed.
k) The nature of the ground can also determine whether support is required during excavation (as for a loose-grained material with a low angle of repose) or whether the support can be provided after completion of the excavation.
l) The ease of removal of the support during the backfilling operation.

4.4 Timbering

Timbering is the method used to support the ground when excavation is done and it is inconvenient or impractical to slope the sides of the excavation back to a safe angle.

Timbers such as deal, pine, fir, or the Baltic red- and whitewoods were and are still used today to provide support to the sides of an excavation. Sheet-steel piling is now frequently used, but is still classed as 'timbering'. In the Standard Method of Measurement, the operation is termed 'planking and strutting'.

The type of timbering required depends on the factors listed in the previous section, but BS 6031:1981, 'Code of practice for earthworks', provides a guide to the general requirements.

a) Terminology

Poling board
: Board varying in length up to 2 m, having a cross-section of approximately 200 mm x 38 mm, placed vertically against the face of the ground.

Trench sheet
: Sheet-steel piles used instead of poling boards.

Waling	Horizontal timber member which supports the poling boards between struts. Size varies from 100 mm x 75 mm to 225 mm x 75 mm.
Struts	Horizontal members holding the poling boards or walings apart, usually placed some 1.8 m to 2 m apart to allow for working room.
Puncheon	Vertical timber member supporting one waling from another in deeper excavations.

b) Open timbering (fig. 4.5)

As the name implies, in open timbering there are gaps between the timbers which support the trench sides, hence the method is suitable only for hard or firm soils.

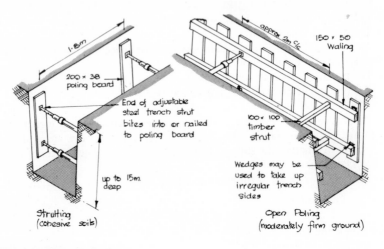

Fig. 4.5 Open timbering

c) Close timbering (fig. 4.6)

In this form of timbering there are no gaps between the timbers supporting the ground, hence this method is used in soft or wet soils.

d) Safety

In all cases of timbering, the work should be carried out in such a way that the operatives installing the timbers are not subject to the risk of trench collapse. They should operate from within the safety of the existing timbering or some cage which effectively protects them.

4.5 Pumping

It may be necessary to remove or exclude water from an excavation so that the work may proceed with the least amount of inconvenience (see section 4.2).

30

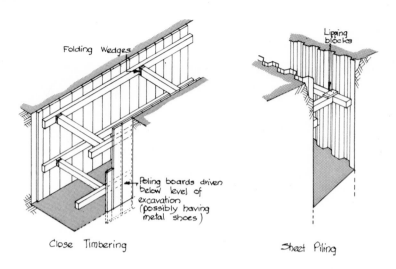

Folding Wedges

Lipping blocks

Poling boards driven below level of excavation (possibly having metal shoes)

Close Timbering

Sheet Piling

Fig. 4.6 Close timbering

There are many sophisticated methods of removing the water from an excavation or preventing its entry, but the most commonly used method is the simplest. This uses a small lift pump or suction pump which draws the water from a sump hole cut below the general level of the excavation, through a rose, which prevents the entry of large particles of muck or stones, up a flexible pipe (50, 75, or 100 mm diameter), and discharges the water through further pipework into the drainage system, a convenient water course, or a distant soakaway (fig. 4.7). This method is suitable for most trench and shallow excavations where the water table or permeability of the strata is not too high. Where this method is unable to cope with the

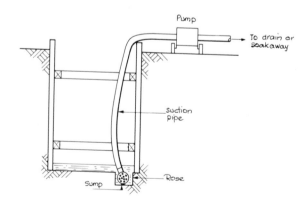

Pump

To drain or soakaway

Suction pipe

Rose

Sump

Fig. 4.7 Trench dewatering by pump

31

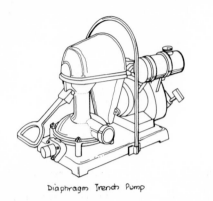

Diaphragm Trench Pump

Centrifugal Self-priming Pump

Fig. 4.8 Pumps

inflow of water, a larger pump or series of pumps may be used (fig. 4.8) or other methods may be employed.

5   Foundations

Understands the applications of typical foundation types and describes their construction.

5.1 Sketches and describes pad and strip foundations for various loads and subsoil conditions.

5.2 Sketches and describes stepped strip foundations and explains the reasons for their use.

5.3 Describes the purpose of steel reinforcement in foundations and indicates its location.

5.4 Sketches and describes a short bored pile foundation and explains the condition under which it may be used.

5.5 Explains the sequence of operations in constructing a short bored pile foundation.

5.6 Sketches and describes the construction of reinforced rigid slabs and pavements.

5.7 Sketches and describes the joints used in 5.6 and explains their function.

Acknowledgement is due to the Technician Education Council for permission to use the content of the TEC units in this chapter. The council reserves the right to amend the content of its units at any time.

5.1 Simple foundations

The Building Regulations 1985, schedule 1, part A, require that 'the building shall be so constructed that the combined dead, imposed and wind loads are sustained and transmitted to the ground safely, and. . . that movements of the subsoil caused by swelling, shrinkage or freezing will not impair the stability of any part of the building.'

Section 2 of approved document A states that the above requirements will be met if the foundations are designed and constructed in accordance with CP 2004: 1972.

However, in section 1 of approved document A, part E, determining the minimum width of strip foundations is simplified by the use of a table. An illustrated abstract from this table is shown in fig. 5.1.

There are further provisions in part E which must be met:

a) The foundations should be situated centrally under the wall.

b) Concrete should be composed of cement to BS 12 and fine and coarse aggregate conforming to BS 882 (i) in the proportion of 50 kg of cement to not more than 0.1 m^3 of fine aggregate and 0.2 m^3 of coarse aggregate, or (ii) grade C15P concrete to BS 5328, or (iii) grade 16 concrete to BS 8110.

Soil Type	Condition	Field Test	Loading	Foundation Detail 250 - 275 cavity wall
II Sand / Gravel } III Clay / Sandy clay }	Compact Stiff	Requires pick for excavation, 50mm square peg hard to drive beyond 150mm deep. Cannot be moulded in the fingers and requires mechanical or pneumatic equipment for its removal.	less than 30 kN/m (typical bungalow)	150 300
II III	— " —	— " —	less than 50 kN/m (Two-storey house)	150 500
II III	— " —	— " —	less than 70 kN/m (three-storey house)	185 650
IV Clay Sandy clay	Firm	Can be moulded by substantial pressure with the fingers and can be excavated by a graft or spade.	less than 30 kN/m	150 360
IV	— " —	— " —	less than 50 kN/m	150 600
IV	— " —	— " —	less than 70 kN/m	285 850
V Sand / Silty sand / Clayey sand Silt / Clay / Sandy clay / Silty clay	Loose Soft	Can be excavated with a spade. 50mm square wooden peg can be easily driven. Fairly easily moulded in the fingers and readily excavated.	less than 30 kN/m	185 650
VII Silt / Clay / Sandy clay / Silty clay	very Soft	Natural sample in winter conditions; exudes between fingers when squeezed in fist.	less than 30 kN/m	285 850

Fig. 5.1 Foundation sizing

c) Minimum thickness of concrete foundations shall be 150 mm or the amount of the projection P (see fig. 5.2), whichever is the greater.

d) Foundations of piers, buttresses, and chimneys should project on all sides to at least the extent of the projection of the associated wall – see fig. 5.2.

A further method of determining strip foundation widths is by the formula

34

$$\text{minimum width} = \frac{\text{total load of wall per metre run}}{\text{bearing capacity of subsoil}}$$

This formula may be adapted for the design of pad foundations:

$$\text{minimum area of pad} = \frac{\text{total load of column}}{\text{bearing capacity of subsoil}}$$

It is usual to have square pads wherever possible, so that the side length can easily be determined. The criteria for depth mentioned in (b) above must still be used since otherwise the foundation will fail as a result of concrete shearing. The depth may be reduced only if a pad containing steel reinforcement is designed (see fig. 5.4).

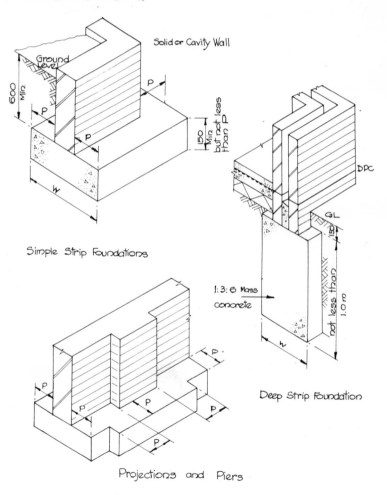

Fig. 5.2 Strip foundations

If the subsoil does not have a suitable bearing strength at the minimum depths below ground level, then further excavation down to more suitable deeper strata will be required. Once the trench has gone down over 1.0 m below the starting point of the excavation, the trench must be made wider to provide more 'elbow' or working room for the men who have to work at those lower levels. However, if the traditional strip-foundation construction (i.e. concrete strip plus brickwork up to the d.p.c. level) can be avoided and no man will have to work in the 'trench', there is no need for additional excavation for width. The deep-strip or narrow-strip or trench-fill foundation was devised for this purpose. The trench is excavated by machine to a suitable strata (400 mm minimum width) and the whole trench is immediately filled with concrete (1:3:6 mix) up to 150 mm below the intended finished ground level. Although expensive in terms of concrete, this method can save money since the costs of excavation, backfill, and timbering are reduced and the whole operation is much faster since bricklaying in the trench is eliminated.

5.2 Stepped foundations

On sloping sites, in order to reduce the amount of excavation, timbering, backfill, and other substructure work — thereby also reducing costs — it is good practice to create a foundation having a series of steps (fig. 5.3). This can be achieved provided that paragraphs E2(e) and E2(f) of section 1 of approved document A of the Building Regulations are complied with: 'Stepped foundations shall overlap by twice the height of the step, the thickness of the foundation, or 300 mm, whichever is the greater. Steps should not be of greater height than the thickness of the foundation.' This ensures the correct transfer of load from the higher to the lower foundation without creating undue excess pressure on the natural foundation.

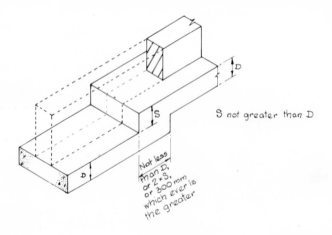

S not greater than D

Not less than D, or 2·S, or 300 mm, which ever is the greater

Fig. 5.3 Stepped foundation

5.3 Reinforced-concrete foundations

It has previously been mentioned that the thickness of the foundation must be equal to the projection from the wall or column if shear failure is to be avoided. However, in the case of a heavily loaded foundation, or on subsoil with a low bearing capacity, large and expensive mass-concrete foundations would be required. A thinner foundation would obviously be more economical, but the concrete, being weak in tension and shear, would have to be strengthened. This strengthening can be achieved by the use of steel reinforcing bars, since steel is strong in tension. The bars are placed in the concrete where the most tension will occur, but they must, in accordance with design requirements, be completely surrounded by a minimum amount of concrete, known as 'cover'. In order to spread the tensile load evenly into the main steel, subsidiary steel bars, called 'distribution steel', are placed at right angles across the main steel. This type of reinforced-concrete foundation is known as a 'wide-strip' foundation (fig. 5.4).

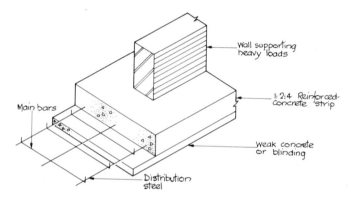

Fig. 5.4 Wide-strip foundation

The correct amount of cover is achieved by placing small precast concrete blocks, whose thickness is equal to the amount of cover required, under the main steel and tying the blocks to the steel so that they do not become dislodged during concreting operations. Other alternatives for maintaining cover include preformed plastics clip-on spacers, wheels, and bent-steel stools, although the last two are specifically used in situations other than simple foundations.

5.4 Short-bored piles

It has already been stated (section 5.1) that a suitable load-bearing stratum must be found for a foundation and that a deep-strip foundation may provide the economic answer. If, however, the depth to a suitable stratum exceeds approximately 1.8 m, trench fill starts to become uneconomic and some other form of foundation must be constructed. 'Short-bored piles' is the name given to a suitable alternative.

A pile is a structural member, usually vertical, which transmits and distributes load from its upper end to the bearing stratum at depth. The distribution of the load takes place (a) by end bearing over the area of the pile base, (b) by adhesion of the surface area of the pile embedded in the bearing strata, or (c) more usually a combination of methods (a) and (b).

The piles support at intervals a reinforced-concrete beam (ground beam) set just below ground level, and this beam in turn supports the walls of the superstructure (fig. 5.5).

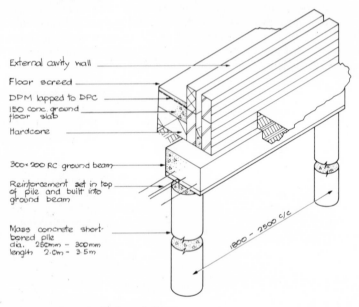

Fig. 5.5 Short-bored-pile foundation

Excavation and concrete content are further reduced by this method, but it is suitable only in shrinkable clay soils which do not contain large stones, boulders, or large tree roots.

5.5 Short-bored-pile construction

The pile holes, which can vary in diameter between 250 mm and 350 mm, are bored by hand or machine auger, the depth bored varying between 1.8 m and 3.5 m depending on ground conditions. Immediately on completion of the excavation, the holes are filled with a 1:2:4-mix concrete to the underneath level of the ground beam, and lengths of reinforcing bar (four per pile) are inserted in the top 600 mm of the pile. The piles are positioned on the centre lines of load-bearing walls, their distribution depending on their load-carrying capacity and the loading from above. There should be piles at

38

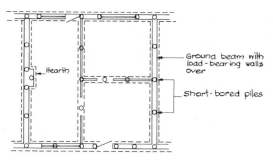

Fig. 5.6 Pile layout

corners, intersections of walls, and other concentrated-load positions such as chimney breasts (fig. 5.6); elsewhere the piles are set at 800 mm to 1.8 m centres.

The ground beam is excavated and a layer of ash, clinker, or weak concrete some 40 to 50 mm thick is placed in the bottom of the trench to cushion any shrinkage or swelling of the clay under the beam. Any necessary formwork is positioned: if the trench has been excavated to the width of the beam and the sides are more or less vertical, then there may be no reason to use formwork; but, if the sides of the trench are unstable and the trench width varies by a large amount, it will be more economical to use forms on account of the savings to be made in the volume of concrete required. If ash or clinker has been used as the blinding, building paper is placed on top of it to prevent a loss of grout from the concrete. Reinforcing bars or a cage are positioned in the trench, the bars from the piles being bent down and linked to the beam reinforcement.

Finally the ground beams are cast, having a smooth level surface on which the brickwork can be laid, and after a suitable period any formwork is removed.

5.6 Reinforced-concrete slabs

Rigid concrete slabs are used in many situations in substructure work, the main ones being raft foundations, solid ground floors, footpaths, and highways. In the majority of instances, the rigidity can be achieved economically only by the use of good-quality concrete and steel reinforcement.

The loading condition will depend upon individual circumstances and, as a result, the slab thickness and amount of reinforcement required will also vary.

The construction of a slab falls into eight distinct sections (fig. 5.7):
a) the subgrade,
b) the sub-base,
c) the formwork,
d) the slip membrane,
e) the joints,

39

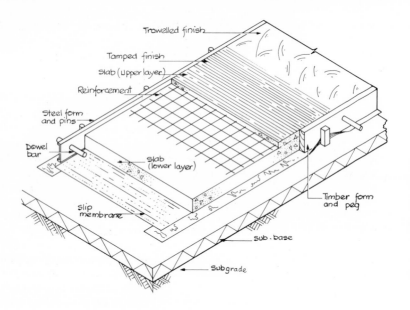

Fig. 5.7 Slab construction

f) the concreting,
g) the finishing,
h) curing.

a) *The subgrade* is the ground from which construction begins, and should be free of topsoil, soft subsoil, hard spots, and large debris.
b) *The sub-base* consists of hardcore and blinding or other suitably graded granular fill which can be fully compacted using hand- or driver-operated vibrating rollers, vibrating plates, or other mechanical compaction equipment.
c) *The side forms,* of timber or preferably steel, are set to the correct line and level on top of a strip of slip membrane some 500 mm wide and are rigidly fixed to the sub-base by steel pins and wedges. Steel road forms with square corners are preferred, since they give good joints and are more rigid and robust than their timber counterparts. They are available in several standard depths and lengths.
   With the side forms correctly positioned, a scratch template is slid along the top of the forms in order to establish the correct level for the sub-base.
d) *The slip membrane,* usually 500-gauge plastics sheeting or building paper, may fulfill a number of functions:
   i) to prevent loss of grout from the concrete to the sub-base;
   ii) to act as a vapour barrier or damp-proof membrane;

40

iii) to permit horizontal movement of the slab without restrictions caused by direct contact with the sub-base.

The membrane is placed on top of the sub-base, the edges of the sheets having 150 mm laps.

e) *The joints* in the slab are discussed in section 5.7.

f) *The concrete* in thin or lightly loaded slabs is laid in two layers, the first layer being poured to a depth some 40 mm below the finished level of the slab. This layer is then compacted down to the level at which the reinforcement is required, any excess being struck off with a notched timber template. The reinforcement, usually thin steel bars spot-welded to form sheets of mesh, having been cut to size, is placed on top of the lower concrete layer with 300 to 450 mm overlap on the previous sheet. The top layer of concrete is spread evenly over the mesh with an approximately 10 mm surcharge above the required level, and the layer is then compacted using a single- or double-beam vibrator (suitable for slab depths up to 150 mm), a poker vibrator (for use where depths exceed 150 mm), or a hand tamper (suitable for depths not exceeding 75 mm) — see fig. 5.8. The layers of concrete should be placed before any initial set has taken place.

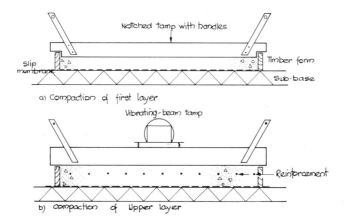

Fig. 5.8 Slab compaction

In the case of thick or heavily loaded slabs, two layers of reinforcement may be required. In this case, ordinary bar reinforcement is used, rather than mesh, and is all positioned prior to pouring of the concrete. The concrete is poured to its full depth (including surcharge) in one pass, followed by compaction as for the thin slab.

Where long lengths of slab are to be formed, such as in road construction, a concrete train or slip-form paver may be used. These machines lay the concrete layers and reinforcing mesh, compact the concrete and provide the required surface finish, and, in the case of the latter machine, provide the side formers and may provide the joints as well.

41

In large floor-slab construction, such as may be required for factories or warehouses, the whole slab is divided into bays, both for ease of construction and in order to reduce the tensile stresses and random cracking caused by thermal and moisture contraction. The width of the bay should not exceed 4.5 m, since this is a size which is suitable for compacting beams to be handled by two men, as well as accepting standard sizes of mesh sheets. There are two types of construction: the conventional chequerboard method and the more economical long-strip method (fig. 5.9). In both cases the infill strips or bays are cast some days after the initial casting, in order to allow the initial concrete to harden sufficiently to withstand the loading caused by the compacting beam.

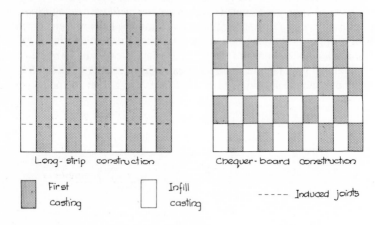

Long-strip construction   Chequer-board construction

First casting   Infill casting   ----- Induced joints

Fig. 5.9 Bay layouts

g) *The finishing* of the slab surface will depend on the intended use of the slab.

The tamped finish or brush finish leaves the slab surface with a series of small ridges which provides a suitable key for a subsequent cement—sand screed, or a good antislip surface on footpaths. The float finish provides a smooth surface.

Use of a wooden float gives the surface a slight roughness which is suitable as an antislip surface in low-traffic areas. A steel float gives a very smooth even surface, and there are several types of steel float avail-

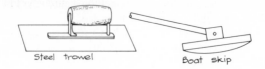

Steel trowel   Boat skip

Fig. 5.10 Hand tools for concrete finishing

able, from the hand trowel through the skip float (fig. 5.10) to the rotating power float.

If a special surface is to be applied to the slab, a better key than that provided by a tamped finish may be required, in which case mechanical scabblers or grinders are used. These machines are also used to expose the aggregate for decorative purposes.

Surface slipperiness may also be reduced by sprinkling natural or metallic aggregates, usually blended with cement, over the slab after initial compaction, before finishing with a power float.

h) *Curing* is essential in producing a hard-wearing slab. The concrete should not be allowed to 'dry out' too quickly or shrinkage cracks will occur. There are several methods of curing:

    i) plastics sheeting is placed on the slab after the initial set has taken place;

    ii) the slab is sprayed with a resin coating after the finish of surface treatment;

    iii) hessian sheeting is placed on the slab as in (i);

    iv) a layer of sand is scattered on the surface after initial set has taken place.

In (i) and (ii), the moisture in the concrete is prevented from evaporating. In the case of (iii) and (iv), the covering must be kept moist so that evaporation occurs from the hessian or sand and not from the concrete.

A stronger surface finish may be obtained by controlling the removal of excess moisture in the concrete by means of rigid or flexible de-watering blankets, especially prior to the use of a power float.

The finish should be protected from damage by keeping foot traffic off the slab for at least 18 hours and wheeled traffic off for at least five days, by covering high-site-traffic areas with hardboard or plywood sheets, and by leaving the plastics curing sheets in place for as long as possible.

5.7 Joints in reinforced-concrete slabs

There are several types of joint used in rigid concrete slabs (fig. 5.11). They are designed to accommodate expansion or contraction of the slab, to

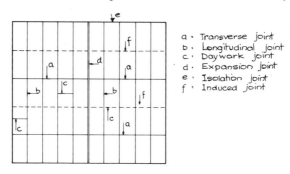

a · Transverse joint
b · Longitudinal joint
c · Daywork joint
d · Expansion joint
e · Isolation joint
f · Induced joint

Fig. 5.11 Joints in slabs

provide a suitable end to a day's pour, or to isolate other fixed parts of the structure. The object of all joints is to reduce the stresses in the concrete which would tend to cause uncontrolled cracking and loss of slab strength.

a) *Traverse control joints*, fig. 5.12(a)   The ends of one bay are tied to the next, but allow contraction to occur. This contraction may result from a drop in the ambient temperature, e.g. from a hot day to a cool night, during the first few days after casting while the concrete is still weak, or it may result from drying shrinkage which does not start until after wet curing and may continue for as long as twelve months.

The tied joint is suitable for most slabs, but for thick slabs and roads the free joint should be used.

In the tied joint, the main reinforcement is kept back some 50 mm from the crack zone while the tying mesh spans the zone by some 250 mm on either side and is supported by spacer blocks. The crack is induced from above by a 5 to 10 mm-wide groove and, where the slab exceeds 200 mm thickness, from below by a triangular-shaped piece of timber or plastics running the full width of the bay.

The free joint, or traverse contraction joint, again has the crack inducers as well as the main steel being curtailed some 50 mm from the

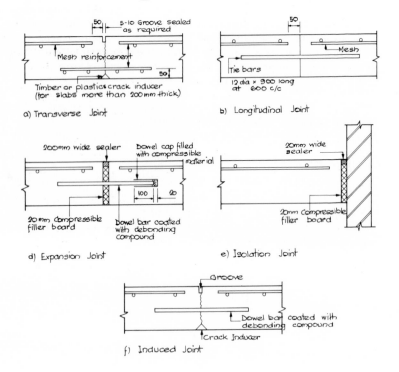

Fig. 5.12 Slab-construction joint details

44

zone, but the slab sections are held in relative position by a dowel bar, positioned at mid-depth, firmly bonded to the slab on one side of the joint and allowing only longitudinal movement by the other section of the slab. The dowel bar is supported by independent cages.

b) *Longitudinal joints*, fig. 5.12(b)   The sides of one bay are tied to the adjacent bays, and long dowel bars are partially inserted through holes in the forms and are cast in with the first bays or strips. After removing the side forms, the remainder of the dowel is cast in with the infill. An alternative method is temporarily to fix one leg of an L-shaped bar to the side of the form so that, after casting and striking the forms, that leg may be cranked out into the adjacent bay before casting of the infill.

c) *Daywork or construction joints*   A traverse joint at the end of the pour, formed exactly as in (b) above.

d) *Expansion joint*, fig. 5.12(d)   Allows thermal expansion of the slab to take place, but is not required at less than 70 m intervals. Dowel bars are used to maintain the relative level of slabs exceeding 150 mm thick, while the movement is taken up by a compressible fibrous filler board some 20 mm thick extending up from the sub-base to some 40 mm below the slab surface. One half of the dowel is coated with a debonding compound such as bitumen or wax, and the end is capped with a plastics or cardboard tube inside which is some compressible material. This allows longitudinal movement of one slab relative to the other. The first slab is cast with the bar bonded into it and the filler board set inside the form. The gap at the top of the filler board is made up with a plastics or timber batten tacked to the form so that a sealing groove is formed on removal. Since it is essential that the expansion movement is not restricted, all the dowels in a bay must be set on the same line, therefore a second drilled former is set away from the first in order to hold the 'free' ends of the dowels in position during the casting of the first slab.

e) *Isolation joint*, fig. 5.12(e)   This allows the floor slab to move without affecting the surrounding walls, internal columns, or machine beds. A filler board, similar to that used in (d) above, is fixed in a similar position against the walls and beds. In the case of steel stanchions it is usual first to cast a rectangular block of concrete from base plate to slab level, and it is to this block that the filler board is attached.

When the whole slab has been cast, the grooves (at contraction, expansion, and isolation joints) are cleaned out and sealed using a hot- or cold-poured bituminous compound, or an extruded flexible-plastics sealing compound.

6   Concreting

Understands the basic principles of concrete production on site.

   *6.1   Lists the materials used in the production of concrete and identifies
          minimum quality standards.*
   6.2   Describes suitable methods of storing concrete materials on site.
   6.3   Describes the batching of concrete by volume and weight.
   *6.4   Describes the effect of water:cement ratio and the consequences of
          inadequate mixing.*
   *6.5   Discusses factors influencing choice between site-mixed and ready-mixed
          concrete.*

Acknowledgement is due to the Technician Education Council for permission to
use the content of the TEC units in this chapter. The council reserves the right to
amend the content of its units at any time.

If good-quality concrete is to be produced, then not only must the constituents of the mix be up to standard — when delivered as well as when used —
but also the equipment used in mixing, transporting, placing, and compacting
must be suitable for the task.

6.1 Materials
The materials used in concrete production are (a) cement, (b) fine aggregate,
(c) coarse aggregate, (d) water, and (e) additives.

a) Cement
There are many varieties of cement available, each meeting a particular need.
   i) *Ordinary Portland cement (OPC)*   A mixture of chalk or limestone and
      clay. The moisture in the initial constituents is driven off by firing the
      materials in a kiln, after which they are ground to a fine powder, with
      gypsum added to control the rate of setting. When the cement comes
      into contact with moisture, a chemical reaction known as hydration
      takes place, causing the material to set and harden. The basic require-
      ments and standard are to be found in BS 12:1978, but simple site tests
      can be carried out as follows:
           place hand into cement and determine if temperature is up to blood
           heat — if it is, then the cement is usable;
           feel the cement for lumps — if it is not of a flour-like consistency, the
           cement has absorbed moisture and is unsuitable for use.
      OPC is suitable for the majority of constructional uses.

ii) *Rapid-hardening cement* (BS 12:1978)   The only difference between rapid-hardening cement and OPC is that the former is more finely ground. The initial set of the materials is similar to OPC, but it subsequently gains strength more rapidly, making it suitable for use where forms must be struck earlier than normal or where there is cold weather in prospect.

iii) *Sulphate-resisting Portland cement* (BS 4027:1980)   Made more resistant to sulphate attack by the reduction of the aluminate content, this cement is frequently used in foundation work, but should not be leaner than a 1:2:4 mix with a minimum water:cement ratio.

iv) *Low-heat Portland cement* (BS 1370:1979)   The amount of heat generated during the hydration process is less than that for OPC. This cement is used in large-mass concrete pours, such as dams, where expansion and contraction cracking is undesirable.

v) *Extra-rapid-hardening Portland cement* (BS 12:1978)
Incorporates an accelerator (calcium chloride) for use in cold weather or where very high early strength is required. Both the rate of hardening (must be placed and compacted within thirty minutes of mixing) and heat generation are increased, but the concrete must still be protected from frost or freezing conditions.

Other more specialist cements include
vi) *Super-sulphated Portland cement*
vii) *Portland blast-furnace cement* (BS 146:part 2:1973)
viii) *Waterproof and water-repellent cements*
ix) *Hydrophobic cement*
x) *Coloured cements*
xi) *Masonry cement*
xii) *High-alumina cement*

b) Fine aggregate (BS 882:1983)

This usually consists of either sand or crushed stone and must pass through a 5 mm BS sieve. The materials should be well graded, i.e. the aggregate should not contain an excess of particles of one particular size. This can be measured using a sieve test and plotting on a graph the percentage mass of a sample passing through a given sieve. The resulting plot can be equated to zones into which sands are classified and which are used for quality control and concrete-mix design. A poorly graded sand or one having a uniform particle size will produce a weak porous concrete with poor workability.

The fine aggregate should be clean. It should not contain any chemical impurities or excessive silt (8% maximum) and should not leave any deposit when rubbed between the fingers. A dirty sand will produce a weak concrete, since there will be a poor bond between the cement and the grains of sand, thus leading to shrinkage cracking.

c) *Coarse aggregate* (BS 882:1983)

Usually gravel, crushed rock, or a combination, this should again be well graded and clean, and also hard, durable, and free from organic materials which might decompose and other impurities such as clay.

Like fine aggregates, coarse aggregates are also graded using sieves complying to BS 410:1976, the methods of testing being outlined in BS 812: part 1:1975.

It should be noted that there is an all-in aggregate available, which is a natural mixture of coarse and fine aggregates, sometimes known as ballast. This material is suitable for mass concrete work where strength is not of great importance, since the proportions of the particle sizes are not constant between one sample and the next.

d) *Water*

If the aggregates are to be clean and free from impurities, so also should be the water.

The most common source of water is the supply-authority mains – this water is ideal for concrete work. However, if there is no mains supply available, tests on the available supply should be carried out (sea water, stream, or well). There is no clear indication of precise levels of impurity in the water which will render it unfit for concreting purposes, but testing two sets of cement cubes in accordance with BS 12 or BS 3148:1980 (one set using the intended water supply, the other set using distilled water) will indicate the compressive strength available and any detrimental effect on the hardening of the concrete.

e) *Additives or admixtures*

These are materials which are added to the concrete mix in order to modify one or more of the properties of the fresh or hardened concrete. There are four main categories:

i) *air-entraining agents,* which improve the workability;

ii) *accelerators,* which reduce the setting time and may promote the early hardening of the mix;

iii) *retarders,* which increase the setting time;

iv) *water-reducers,* which reduce the permeability of the concrete and increase the strength without loss of workability.

BS 5075:part 2:1982 covers the standards required for category (i), and BS 5075:part 1:1982 covers categories (ii), (iii), and (iv).

6.2 Storage

The materials used in the production of concrete should be up to the required standard when delivered to the site, and, if the concrete produced is to be of good quality, those materials should be stored in such a way that their quality is not impaired before use.

a) *Cement*   Cement is supplied in bulk, in bags, or in drums. Bulk cement is delivered to site by tanker and is blown into storage silos by compressed air. The silo, sited alongside the mixer, is used when large volumes of concrete are to be produced. It consists of a metal cylinder approximately 5 m high and 3 m in diameter having a base in the form of an inverted cone from which the cement is discharged into an automatic weighing hopper. This hopper may be swung or slid out and the cement discharged into the hopper of the mixer. The whole silo, set in an elevated position, is sealed to prevent the entry of moisture from the atmosphere.

Bagged cement, delivered on a waggon having a tarpaulin cover, should be stored in a closed cabin, the floor of which is at least 150 mm above the ground (fig. 6.1). The bags should be stacked closely together, to prevent the circulation of air around them, but not higher than 1.5 m,

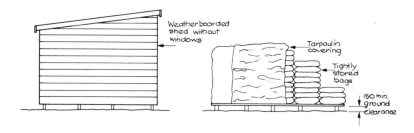

Fig. 6.1 Cement storage

and in such a manner that the cement is used in the same order as that in which it was received. Different types of cement should not be stored together. If a cabin is not available, the bags should be stored on boards raised above the ground and be covered by waterproof covers having large overlaps.

Cement in drums will last for an indefinite period provided the seal on the lid is not damaged.

b) and c) *Aggregate*   Aggregate should be stored in bins or hoppers so that the stockpiles do not mix. The storage should have a clean hard base with adequate drainage – this will prevent contamination from the ground below, as well as reducing the moisture content of the aggregate. (The moisture content of the aggregate will affect the amount of water to be added to the mix.) The aggregates are usually stored radially in bags or bins around the mixer (fig. 6.2), but, where automatic batching is carried out, a series of in-line hoppers is used in conjunction with a conveyor-belt system. The storage area should be kept away from trees, in order to avoid any airborne contamination.

d) *Water*   The mains water or other supply may not be directly available at the mixer, and any method of storage should maintain the quality of the water and not pollute it.

e) *Admixtures*   These are usually delivered in cartons or drums, which should be clearly marked and kept separate from each other.

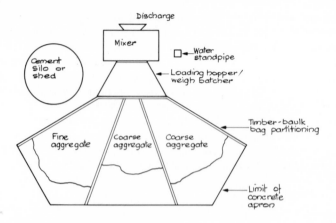

Fig. 6.2 Plan of radial materials storage

6.3 Batching

Concrete is now graded by its characteristic strength and subsequently the situation in which it is to be used (BS 8110:part 1:1985), fig. 6.3 (see also BS 5328:1981).

The concrete mix is specified by proportions of the cement, fine aggregate, and coarse aggregate, and these proportions may be stated in terms of mass (fig. 6.4) or volume (fig. 6.5) mass being the more commonly used.

There are, however, nominal mixes which are widely used in the building industry where the proportions are whole numbers; e.g. a 1:2:4 mix means one part of cement to two parts of fine aggregate to four parts of coarse

Grade	Characteristic compressive strength (N/mm^2)	Min. cement content (kg/m^3)	Appropriate use
C7.5	7.5	120	Plain concrete
C10	10.0	150	Plain concrete
C15	15.0	180	Plain concrete
C15	15.0	240	Reinforced concrete with lightweight aggregate
C25	25.0	240	Reinforced concrete with normal-weight aggregate
C30	30.0	300	Post-tensioned concrete
C40	40.0	300	Pre-tensioned concrete

Fig. 6.3 Recommended grades of concrete (from BS 8110)

Nominal max. size of aggregate (mm)		40		20	
Workability		Medium	High	Medium	High
Concrete	Range of slump (mm)	50–100	80–170	25–75	65–135
C7.5	Total aggregate (kg)	1080	920	900	780
	Fine aggregate (%)	30–45	30–45	35–50	35–50
C10	Total aggregate (kg)	900	800	770	690
	Fine aggregate (%)	30–45	30–45	35–50	35–50
C15	Total aggregate (kg)	790	690	680	580
	Fine aggregate (%)	30–45	30–45	35–50	35–50
C25	Total aggregate (kg)	560	510	510	460
	Sand: zone 1 (%)	35	40	40	45
	zone 2 (%)	30	35	35	40
	zone 3 (%)	30	30	30	35
C30	Total aggregate (kg)	510	460	460	400
	Sand: zone 1 (%)	35	40	40	45
	zone 2 (%)	30	35	35	40
	zone 3 (%)	30	30	30	35

Fig 6.4 Proportions of dry aggregates to be used with 100 kg of cement (from BS 5328)

aggregate; a 1:5 mix indicates one part of cement to five parts of all-in aggregate.

A batch is the amount of materials required for one mixing of concrete, either by hand or, preferably, by mechanical means.

Batching by mass is usually carried out using a hopper linked to a weighing dial. Fixed pointers are set around the dial so that the correct masses of the mix constituents are placed in the hopper, the sequence of loading being as follows: half the total mass of coarse aggregate, total mass of fine aggregate, total mass of cement, followed by the remainder of the coarse aggregate. The batch is loaded into the mixer simultaneously with the required amount of water.

Batching by volume is generally used for small amounts of concrete mixed by hand or in a small mixer which does not incorporate a hopper feed. The batch is based on a mix containing a bag (50 kg) of cement, fig. 6.5. A gauge box (also known as a batch box or measuring frame) is used to measure out the aggregates. The box should be deep and narrow, hold the full amount of the required batch or an exact fraction ($\frac{1}{2}$ or $\frac{1}{4}$), and be no larger than about 0.05 m^3 (approx. 300 mm x 400 mm x 417 mm deep) since above this size it will be difficult to handle. If the mixing is being carried out by hand, it should be done on a clean, smooth, hard, level surface. In this case, the gauge box need not have a level base.

Mix	Cement	Sand	Coarse aggregate	Use
1 : 3 : 6	50 kg bag	0.10 m³	0.20 m³	Mass concrete work, foundations, ground floors
1 : 2 : 4	"	0.07 m³	0.14 m³	General reinforced-concrete work
1 : 1½ : 3	"	0.05 m³	0.10 m³	Watertight or very strong concrete

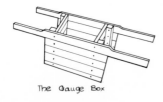

The Gauge Box

The Shovel Full?

Fig. 6.5 Mix proportions by volume

The box is filled with aggregate and the surplus is struck off with a straight edge for accuracy. The quantities shown in fig. 6.5 are for dry materials, and a suitable allowance should be made if the sand is damp, since it bulks (increases in volume).

In taking the aggregate from the storage area, care must be taken to ensure that a properly graded batch is used. This means that the material should not be taken from the top or bottom of the stockpile, since the large particles tend to fall to the base leaving the fine material at the top.

6.4 Water:cement ratio

A batch of concrete should contain the minimum amount of water necessary to provide sufficient workability for the full compaction of the concrete while at the same time not greatly impairing the strength of the concrete.

The amount of water present in a mix is defined in terms of the water:cement ratio. This ratio is

$$\frac{\text{the total mass of water}}{\text{mass of cement}}$$

The total mass of water is the sum of the mass of water added to the mix and the amount of water present in the batched aggregates (i.e. their moisture content).

A water:cement ratio of approximately 0.25 is required to achieve full hydration of the mix (12 kg or 12 litres per 50 kg bag of cement). This ratio will produce the highest strength of concrete from the batch but will give inadequate workability. A water:cement ratio of less than 0.5 will produce a concrete which is difficult to compact by hand. A ratio of about 0.42 is suitable for good-quality concrete giving reasonable workability using mechanical compaction methods. Figure 6.6 shows the relationship between strength and water:cement ratio.

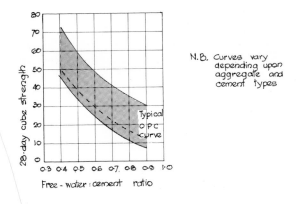

Fig. 6.6 Graph showing strength as a function of water:cement ratio

The degree of workability can be tested on site by several methods, the easiest being the slump test, which also gives an indication of the water:cement ratio and the consistency of various batches.

A hollow metal mould, shown in fig. 6.7, is filled with concrete in four layers, each approximately ¼ of the height of the mould. Each layer is tamped 25 times with the tamping rod in a uniform manner over the area of the mould. After the top layer has been tamped, the concrete is struck off level with the top of the mould, which is then slowly lifted clear of the concrete. The cone of concrete will subside and slump. The upended cone

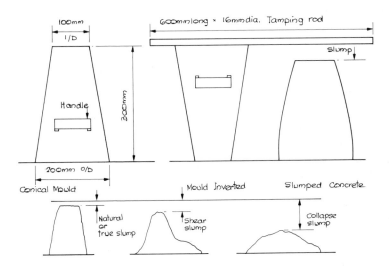

Fig. 6.7 Slump test

is placed alongside the concrete and the slump (difference in level between the top of mould and the top of the concrete) is measured.

The batch should be thoroughly mixed. Evidence of this is provided by the development of a uniform colour and consistency (two minutes in a rotating-drum mixer being considered adequate — longer for low-workability mixes). Failure to achieve thorough mixing will result in pockets of aggregate not being coated with cement, which produces weak areas in the concrete, giving inconsistent strength.

6.5 Choosing ready-mixed or site-mixed concrete
The choice between the use of ready-mixed or site-mixed concrete is made on the basis of the advantages and disadvantages of each method of production in the particular situation.

Ready-mixed concrete
Advantages
a) No space is required on site for the mixer and storage of materials. This is especially beneficial on a small or restricted site.
b) A smaller amount of concrete-transportation plant is required.
c) A smaller labour force is required.
d) Quality control of the materials and concrete is the responsibility of the ready-mixed-concrete supplier. If a strength mix is ordered, the supplier can, with the knowledge of the materials used, generally produce a more economic mix than by site batching. Any costs incurred as a result of a poor-quality strength mix are also recoverable from the supplier.
e) Economic for medium-volume requirements.
Disadvantages
a) Good access is required, appropriate to the size and weight of the ready-mixed-concrete transporter.
b) Delivery may be difficult to obtain on account of (a).
c) Concrete should be ordered the day before it is required. In cases where a large volume is required on a specific day, more than one day's notice may be required.
d) There is no check (other than by delivery ticket) on the quantities delivered.
e) If a delivery vehicle is not discharged within a given period, an additional fee is chargeable.
f) Vehicles delivering part loads are uneconomical.

Site-mixed concrete
Advantages
a) The contractor has control of the quality of all materials as well as of the end product.
b) Concrete can be available when required, even at very short notice.

c) Any quantity of material can be supplied (limited only by the output capacity of the mixer).
d) Smaller access routes for distribution are required than for ready-mix waggons.
e) Economic for large- or small-volume requirements.

Disadvantages
a) Space required to set up plant and storage areas.
b) Cost of setting up and maintaining plant and storage areas.
c) No come-back if poor-quality concrete is produced.
d) Regular quality control must be carried out.
e) Good access must be provided for the delivery of the cement and aggregates.
f) Plant is required for the distribution of the concrete.
g) Skilled operatives must be employed for the batching and mixing processes.

On a large site requiring the production of vast quantities of concrete, the contractor may set up his own central ready-mixed batching plant and enjoy the advantages of both systems of production.

7   Formwork

Understands the basic principles of formwork construction.

7.1   Identifies the principal requirements of formwork construction and its associated terminology.

7.2   Sketches and describes simple formwork construction and explains sequence of operations for erection and striking.

Acknowledgement is due to the Technician Education Council for permission to use the content of the TEC units in this chapter. The council reserves the right to amend the content of its units at any time.

Formwork, sometimes known as shuttering or casing, is the boarding or sheeting which is erected to contain and mould the wet concrete during placing and the initial hardening period. It accounts for a substantial part of the cost of the finished concrete — in extreme cases, perhaps as much as 75%. In Britain it is general practice for the structural consultant to design the concrete structure, but the design of the formwork is left to the contractor — on large-scale concrete operations, the contractor may be required to submit his formwork design to the consultants for approval.

There are two types of formwork, namely *permanent* and *temporary*. The permanent is that which will remain in place after the concreting operation. This may be because of the impracticability of its removal once the work has been completed, or due to a finished facing material having been used as the formwork in the first instance.

7.1 Formwork requirements
The requirements of formwork construction are
a) strength,
b) rigidity,
c) tightness,
d) good alignment,
e) surface finish,
f) durability,
g) ease of placing concrete,
h) ease of stripping,
j) economy.

a) The formwork should be strong enough to carry safely the dead weight of the wet concrete placed on it, together with the live loading from the men and machines used in placing the concrete in position and the impact loading caused by the concrete being discharged into the formwork.

b) There should be sufficient rigidity in the formwork to maintain the correct lines and levels without undue bulging or sagging. This may be achieved by the use of additional props at critical points.

c) The joints between sections of formwork should be sufficiently tight as to prevent the loss of water or grout from the contained concrete. If such a loss occurs, a weakness may be caused in the concrete at that point, together with surface blemishes on the finished unit. The joints may be sealed by the use of foamed plastics or adhesive tape.

d) The joints between forms should be smooth, so that no unwanted surface irregularities are apparent on the finished unit.

e) The surface-finish requirement for the concrete may be smooth, textured, or of exposed aggregate. These finishes may be achieved by the use of different surfaces on the formwork and may dictate the materials to be used for the formwork.

f) The forms should be designed to be strong and rigid enough not only in use but also for handling and stripping purposes as well, since durable formwork is also economic.

g) In designing the formwork and the amount of concrete to be placed or poured at any one time, the ease with which the operation can be carried out must be taken into account.

h) Although it is one of the last operations in the casting process, the ease with which the formwork can be stripped is of paramount importance. It is at this stage that much time and expense can be saved and the likelihood of damage to the newly cast work be reduced.

j) The contractor is interested in keeping his shuttering costs to a minimum, and the correct use of the materials used and their repeated re-use in a correct manner will assist in achieving this economy. A shutter should be re-used as many times as possible — using timber forms a minimum of ten times should be aimed for — and the design aim should be for the form to fit as many standard situations as possible with little or no modification. The method of jointing one shutter with the next should also be standardised and designed on the grounds of economy, not only from the usage point of view, but also to minimise the time taken for erection and stripping of the forms.

Terminology

Bearers	Those horizontal members which support the joists and transfer the loading to the props or posts.
Clamp	Metal anchorage used to hold formwork in position (generally formwork to walls, deep beams, and columns).
Cleats	i) Vertical framing members behind the form face in wall forms.

ii) Temporary anchorages for other items of formwork.

Decking	The horizontal form face to slab soffits.
Joist	Horizontal member supporting the decking.
Ledgers	See 'Bearers'.
Prop	i) Vertical member supporting the higher level formwork and transferring the load to a stable base. ii) Inclined member holding vertical formwork plumb.
Runner	A horizontal member, similar to a bearer, which supports the joists.
Sheeting	See 'Decking'.
Soldier	Strong stiff vertical member supporting and anchoring vertical forms.
Spacers	Small timber or steel members which keep the form faces the correct distance apart in wall and beam forms.
Spanforms	Steel joists having adjustable length.
Striking	The removal of the formwork from the faces of the cast concrete.
Stripping	See 'Striking'.
Struts	Compression members designed to hold the formwork stable.
Ties	Steel bolts or wires which anchor the form faces in vertical work together — generally used in conjunction with spacers.
Yokes	Timber clamps around column shutters.

7.2 Simple formwork construction

Formwork must be designed taking into account all the requirements stated in the previous sections.

There are two components to formwork: the face which comes into contact with the concrete and the support behind that face (fig. 7.1).

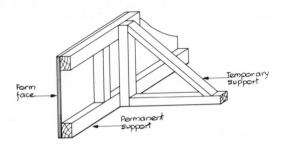

Fig. 7.1 Formwork components

Form face

The face of the form will in the majority of cases determine the surface finish of the concrete. A permeable facing will allow water to pass from the wet concrete to the form, and this water carries with it the smaller particles of cement. These particles, however, being too large to pass with the water through the facing, are deposited at the surface of the concrete. This gives a denser mix at the surface of the concrete, with an inherent darker colour. As it is practically impossible to obtain an even movement of water through the form face, marked variations in the colour of the finished concrete can and do occur.

An impermeable facing, particularly one with a polished surface, gives rise to blow holes (very small holes caused by bubbles of air being trapped against the surface of the form). This type of facing used in conjunction with a wet mix of concrete will cause crazing of the surface, which on exposed surfaces will fill with grime and atmospheric pollutants, creating a more pronounced ageing effect.

There are several materials used for facing the forms:

a) *Hardboard* (not oil-tempered)   This material is not of uniform consistency and absorbancy, and therefore will give colour variation on the finished concrete surface. On the first usage it will give a surface reasonably free from blow holes, but on subsequent usages it will become more and more impermeable as cement and release agents seal the surface.

b) *Hardboard* (oil-tempered)   Almost impermeable, this material will give the concrete a uniform surface colour, but with inevitable blow holes.

c) *Plywood and timber*   The nature of the natural materials can cause many problems. Permeability may vary from the impermeable heartwood to the permeable sapwood across the growth rings, and may also depend on the angle at which the timber was cut. As with hardboard, wide colour variation in the finished concrete can occur, and the incidence of blow holes will also increase with usage as the timber becomes sealed. However, plywood with its cross-grained structure provides a strong and reasonably economic facing.

d) *Steel*   This produces concrete of uniform colour when protected from rust, but there will be the inevitable blow holes resulting from the impermeable surface. Good maintenance can ensure that this type of form is re-used many times.

e) *Plastics and glass fibre.* These materials produce an effect on the concrete similar to that of steel, but there is also a tendency for them to produce crazing.

The support

The support behind the face may be divided into two categories: permanent and temporary. When standard forms are being used they will usually have the face set on a permanent supporting framework. This is usually made from wood or steel, but in the case of plastics and glass-fibre facing it may be incorporated in the moulding in the form of ribs and angles.

The temporary support consists of the props, soldiers, ledgers, joists, runners, and all other equipment which holds the forms in position and transfers the loading from the form to the ground or other part of the structure.

Release agents

In order to facilitate the striking or removal of the formwork, and to prevent the concrete adhering to the form face, the face should be thoroughly cleaned of concrete, mud, and other matter and, immediately prior to erection, be coated with a release agent. These agents will also reduce the amount of form face adhering to the concrete surface. (The method of cleaning will also play a part in determining the number of re-uses obtained from a form.)

Most oils will fulfil the function of a release agent, but different oils can produce blow holes or variations in the colour of the concrete, affect efflorescence, or retard the hardening of the surface of the concrete, causing a rough exposed-aggregate finish.

There are a number of release agents available which can be classified as follows.

a) *Neat oils*   Most mineral and vegetable oils induce the formation of air bubbles, thus giving blow holes. These oils are not recommended for quality work.

b) *Neat oils with surfactant added*   A surfactant is a surface-wetting agent which gives a uniform spread of oil on the form face, hence reducing blow holes. The amount of surfactant should not exceed 2% by volume, otherwise the surface hardening of the concrete will be impaired.

c) *Mould-cream emulsions* (emulsions of water in oil)   Neat oil and water are combined with a surfactant to form an emulsion of water globules in oil. The preparation acts as (b) above, but is suitable for good-quality work.

d) *Water-soluble emulsions* (emulsions of oil in water)   These act as (b) but contain a higher percentage of surfactant and are therefore not suitable for quality work.

e) *Chemical release agents*   There are many branded products on the market and, while the majority can produce very good results, site trials should be carried out to test the results in given sets of circumstances.

f) *Paints and varnishes*   These are not strictly release agents — they act only as an impermeable surface on the form. A release agent should be used with this finish, and care must be taken to select a paint or varnish which is compatible with the form material, alkali-resistant, hard, durable, and not affected by the release agent.

Erection

Beams   The shuttering to concrete beams (reinforced or not) may be supported in a number of ways (fig. 7.2), but the three main methods are:

a) using timber props,
b) using adjustable steel props,
c) using scaffolding to support adjustable fork heads.

The shuttering to steel beams (where a concrete surround is given for fire-protection purposes) may be supported as described above, but, provided that the steelwork is properly anchored, it may also be suspended from the steelwork itself.

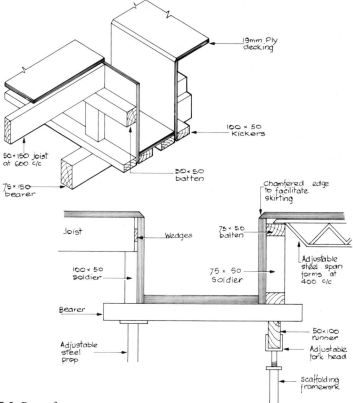

19mm Ply decking

100 × 50 Kickers

50 × 150 joist at 600 c/c

75 × 150 bearer

50 × 50 batten

Chamfered edge to facilitate skirting

Joist

Wedges

75 × 50 batten

100 × 50 Soldier

75 × 50 Soldier

Adjustable steel span forms at 400 c/c

Bearer

50 × 100 runner

Adjustable fork head

Adjustable steel prop

Scaffolding framework

Fig. 7.2 Beam forms

The design of the shuttering should allow the slab and beam side forms to be removed while the beam soffit remains supported. The reason for this is that the beam is a major load-bearing member and is required to have more strength than the surrounding floors. Since it will be immediately carrying the floor weight, its own weight, and any further loading applied to the floor, that strength must already have been achieved when the temporary support is removed.

Columns   The shuttering for columns can be made from plywood, timber, plastics, glass fibre, pitch fibre, steel.

61

Columns are usually square or circular in section, but those of materials other than timber find their best application in the circular shapes and usually consist of two halves which are flanged and bolted together.

Before casting an in-situ column, it is usual to cast a column starter approximately 75 mm high, either integral with the floor slab or while the floor-slab concrete is 'green'. This starter is known as the *kicker* (fig. 7.3).

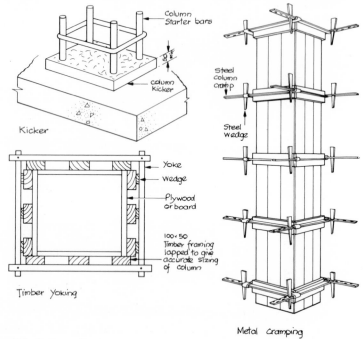

Fig. 7.3 Column forms

The kicker serves two purposes: (a) to position accurately the base of the column and (b) to act as an anchorage against upthrust for the column shuttering.

Since wet concrete acts, to some extent, in a similar manner to water, the shuttering must be able to withstand the hydraulic pressure exerted on it by the poured concrete. For this reason, the column shutter supports near the base of the form should be closer together than those at the head of the column (remember, pressure increases with depth).

Once the formwork is erected, it should be checked for verticality with an offset plumb-bob and be securely braced.

To prevent segregation of the concrete when pouring high columns, it may be necessary to incorporate a trap door in the shuttering at approximately the mid-point in height of the column, thereby allowing concrete to be placed without it dropping full height. The alternative is to pour the concrete from the top of the form using a tremie pipe.

Slabs Formwork to suspended slabs is similar to that for beams, except that the soffit shuttering is far wider — usually formed by standard-size (2.4 m × 1.2 m) plywood sheets (fig. 7.4).

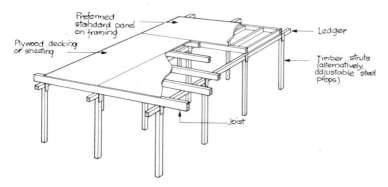

Fig. 7.4 Slab forms

In the case of ground-floor slabs, the hardcore and blinding form a permanent soffit shutter while the brickwork of the walls provides a permanent vertical side shutter.

Striking

This is the reverse process to erection. Before formwork can be removed the concrete must have

a) sufficient *strength* to support itself — this may be after 30 minutes or after 28 days, depending on the concrete mix, the water:cement ratio, and the situation of the concrete;

b) sufficient *surface hardness* to resist damage — damage can be caused by using the concrete to lever off the forms, by impact from site vehicles and falling objects, or by passing pedestrian traffic;

c) sufficient *curing* to give a reasonable colour finish to the concrete — too soon as exposure to the atmosphere will cause discoloration. For quality work where appearance is important, formwork should not be removed until at least four days after pouring or as shown in the table (fig. 7.5), whichever is the longer.

	Surface temperature of concrete	
	7°C	16°C and above
Vertical formwork to columns, walls, and large beams	18 hours	12 hours
Soffit formwork to slabs	6 days	4 days
Soffit formwork to beams and props to slabs	15 days	10 days
Props to beams	21 days	14 days

Fig. 7.5 Periods before formwork should be removed from OPC concrete (from BS 8110)

8 External walls

Understands the construction of external walls and formation of openings.

8.1 Describes further examples of bonding and factors affecting choice of bond.

8.2 Explains functions of attached piers.

8.3 Sketches and describes typical parapet walls and identifies functions.

8.4 Describes the use of damp-proof courses and membranes.

8.5 Sketches and describes means of providing support over openings.

8.6 Sketches and describes methods of constructing arches over openings.

8.7 Sketches and describes typical details at head, sill, and jambs.

Acknowledgement is due to the Technician Education Council for permission to use the content of the TEC units in this chapter. The council reserves the right to amend the content of its units at any time.

8.1 Further bonding

Walls constructed of bricks or blocks are bonded for strength, and examples of simple bonding for $\frac{1}{2}$- and 1-brick walls were detailed in Volume 1, section 8.4.

The loading on a wall may be such as to require a wall thickness greater than one brick. This may lead to complications in the layout of a bond, as with the junction of one wall with another other than at corners, or the formation of an opening.

In order to relieve the monotony of a bonded wall, features may be incorporated: patterns established using differently coloured bricks or bricks projected forward from the main face.

In general, the choice of bond is determined by the function the wall has to perform, its situation in the building, and its thickness.

Further examples of bonding are shown in figs 8.1 to 8.3.

8.2 Piers

A pier is a column of masonry. It may be free-standing or attached to a wall.

An attached pier is positioned to carry heavy point or concentrated loads such as a main beam, truss, or arch (fig. 8.4). Instead of or in addition to its load-carrying function, it may also provide stability to a wall — especially a $\frac{1}{2}$-brick wall.

In approved document A (clause C26) of the Building Regulations 1985, the provision of a pier or buttressing wall to another wall has the effect of dividing that wall into sections when considering the structural stability of that wall. In the case of $\frac{1}{2}$-brick wall for a garage whose length is 5.5 m, an attached pier would be required in such a position that the length of the wall from front or back to pier would not exceed 3 m. The width of a pier should be three times the wall thickness and in no case less than 190 mm, unless it is for the wall of a single-storey outbuilding such as a garage.

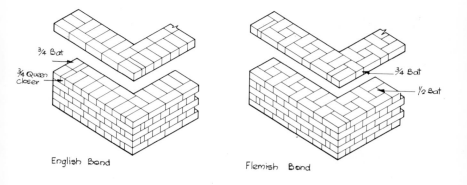

Fig. 8.1 Bonding at quoin of $1\frac{1}{2}$-brick wall

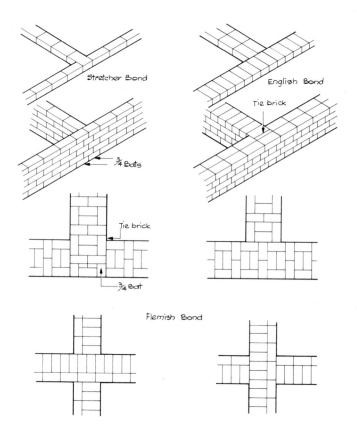

Fig. 8.2 Bonding of walls at junctions

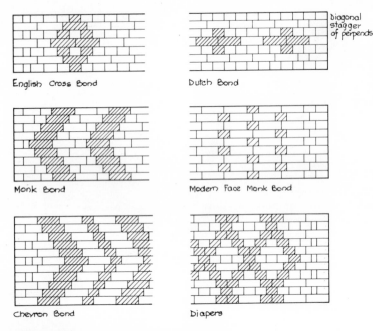

English Cross Bond

Dutch Bond

Diagonal stagger of perpends

Monk Bond

Modern Face Monk Bond

Chevron Bond

Diapers

Fig. 8.3 Bonding for features and patterns

The brickwork of the pier is securely bonded into the wall by headers which project from the pier into the wall or vice versa.

8.3 Parapets

A parapet wall is a low wall which guards the edge of a roof, balcony, terrace, or bridge. It projects a small distance above the main structure and is exposed to the elements on its face, back, and top. The wall must be carefully detailed so as to prevent the entry of moisture into the structure below, In accordance with the Building Regulations 1985, approved document A, clause C11 and Table C4, the minimum thickness of a parapet and its maximum height from the level of the junction of the wall and structural roof shall be:

		Wall thickness (mm)	Max. height of parapet (mm)
a) Cavity walls:			
sum of thicknesses of leaves	i)	200 max.	600
	ii)	201–250	860
b) Solid walls	i)	150	600
	ii)	190	760
	iii)	215	860

The thickness of the parapet should not be greater than that of the wall supporting it. Higher parapets should be designed in accordance with BS 6180 and BS 5628.

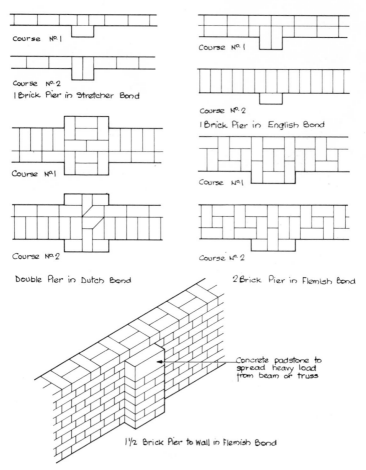

Course No. 1

Course No. 2
1 Brick Pier in Stretcher Bond

Course No. 1

Course No. 2
1 Brick Pier in English Bond

Course No. 1

Course No. 2
Double Pier in Dutch Bond

Course No. 1

Course No. 2
2 Brick Pier in Flemish Bond

Concrete padstone to spread heavy load from beam or truss

1½ Brick Pier to Wall in Flemish Bond

Fig. 8.4 Details of attached piers

In the case of a solid construction, the top of the wall is finished off by means of a coping made of precast or in-situ concrete; slate; sheet lead, copper, or zinc; or brick on edge (fig. 8.5). In cavity construction, a precast concrete coping is generally used.

Damp-proof courses are used to prevent the entry of moisture to the lower levels, and their use is of prime importance in cavity construction where the parapet extends above roof level. In this case, the back leaf of the parapet becomes the inner leaf of the wall below roof level, and moisture is prevented from reaching the lower levels by the use of a stepped d.p.c. with weep holes provided at intervals in the back leaf immediately above the d.p.c. (fig. 8.6). It is also essential that the roof or other surface covering is tucked under or flashed to the lowest d.p.c. in the parapet wall, in order to prevent entry of moisture to the roof structure or lower walls.

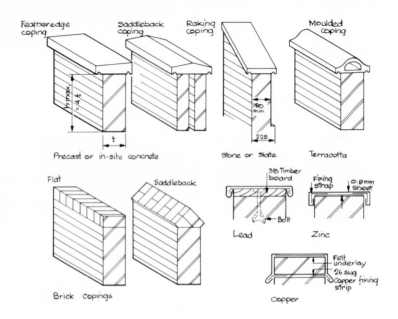

Fig. 8.5 Parapet copings

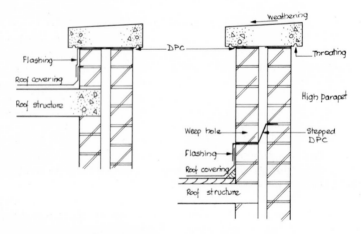

Fig. 8.6 Damp-proofing parapets

8.4 Damp-proof courses

It was stated in Volume 1 that a damp-proof course prevents the upward movement of moisture from the ground by breaking the capillary attraction in the material of the wall. However, capillary attraction acts not only vertically upwards but also in all directions. Therefore, wherever there is a contact between the external and internal leaves of a cavity wall, an impermeable barrier or d.p.c. must be incorporated in such a way that no moisture may penetrate to the inside surfaces of a building.

Openings in the external envelope for doors, windows, chimneys, or pipework and the construction of parapet walls are the most common places where there is likely to be an entry of water from the outside to the inside of the building, and it is in these situations (fig. 8.7) that d.p.c.'s are commonly used in addition to the situation already described, i.e. just above ground level.

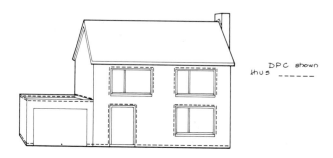

DPC shown thus _ _ _ _ _ _

Fig. 8.7 Damp-proof-course location

The requirements of a d.p.c. are that it be impermeable, flexible, semi-rigid or rigid, and capable of withstanding the loads imposed on it without deformation or loss of impermeability. Flexible materials such as lead, copper, bituminous felt, and polythene are suitable for most situations, especially around openings. Semi-rigid materials such as asphalt are suitable for use in thick walls, where the width of standard flexible materials would generally require laps to be made. Rigid materials such as slate or engineering bricks are ideal in horizontal situations where heavy loading occurs, but care must be taken to ensure that any structural movement will not fracture this type of damp-proof course.

Damp-proof membranes are used at roof and ground level and could be considered as damp-proof courses covering a much larger area. The membranes are generally formed using those materials mentioned above as being suitable for flexible and semi-rigid d.p.c.'s. It is generally the case that d.p.m.'s should be lapped with or flashed to a d.p.c.

8.5 Openings

An opening in a wall consists of a head, a jamb or reveal, and a threshold or sill (fig. 8.8).

There is generally some load to be supported above the head — in the form of a wall, roof, floor, or any combination of these — and there should therefore be some form of beam provided across the top of the opening

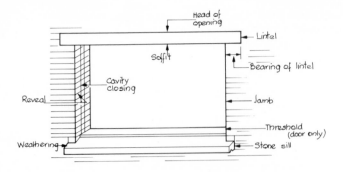

Fig. 8.8 Opening terminology

which will carry the loading without undue deflection, since the framework of the window itself is designed to support only the glass and any wind loading.

Historically, the head of a window opening was in the form of an arch well before the flat beam or lintel came into use. The construction of the arch is more fully described in the next section.

There are several forms of lintel which may be used (fig. 8.9), and they may be classified either by material or by whether they are concealed or exposed. It should be noted at this stage that any lintel should have adequate bearing or seating (minimum 100 mm) on the sides or jambs of the opening, so that the weight carried by the lintel is transferred to the wall without undue stress being created in either.

a) *Timber*   Suitable for internal use, but also occasionally used in external walls; in both cases should be used only for small spans (2 m maximum) with light loading conditions. When used externally, it should be well treated with preservative.

b) *Concrete*   (in-situ or precast)   Since tension will be developed in the bottom of the beam, reinforcement will be required. The concrete lintel can be designed to span most distances, but it must be remembered that the use of precast lintels will be limited by the ease with which they may be lifted into position.

c) *Steel*   There is a vast range of shapes used for lintels in a wide variety of situations. For small spans, a mild-steel flat or angle is suitable for supporting the outer leaf of a cavity wall. Alternatively, a specially pre-formed section will support both leaves of a cavity wall over small and medium spans (up to 4.5 m). For large spans, the standard rolled sections (channel and beam) are selected after design calculations.

d) *Brick*   Special bricks may be used to form a flat arch (fig. 8.10), but the strength of the arch will support only a single skin over spans of about 1 m. Additional strength is obtained by providing support from other lintel forms, or by the use of brick reinforcements in the horizontal bed joint some two or three courses above the opening.

70

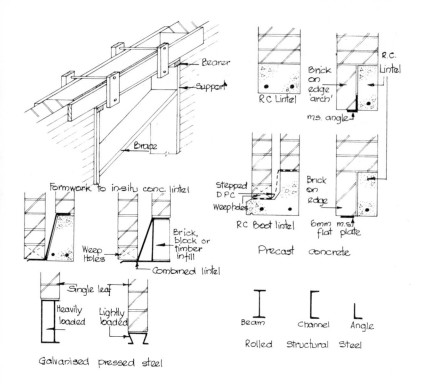

Fig. 8.9 Lintels

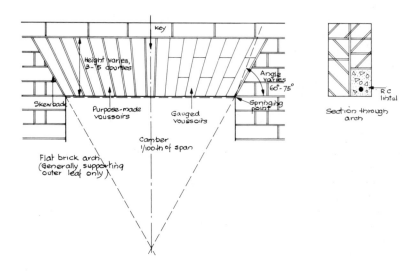

Fig. 8.10 Details of a flat arch

71

e) *Stone*   In its many forms, stone is seldom used independently of any other material in forming a lintel. It is more usual to use it in a similar manner to bricks, i.e. as a facing to a steel or concrete lintel.

8.6 Arches
Arches in stone or brick are nowadays seldom used because of cost, but in the eighteenth and nineteenth centuries they were very popular and they have a terminology all of their own (fig. 8.11).

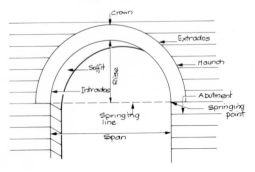

Fig. 8.11   Arch terminology

Arches are generally classified by their shape (flat, segmental, or semi-circular) and are formed using either plain bricks, cut or axed bricks, purpose-made bricks, or rubbers (soft red bricks which can easily be sawn or rubbed to the required shape).

In forming the arch, the bricks or stones require support not only during construction until the key brick or stone is inserted – the arch is constructed from both springing points upwards and the key brick is the last item to be laid – but also until the mortar joints are strong enough to support not only the weight of the arch but also the weight of wall being built on top. This support is known as centring (fig. 8.12) and is formed using small-section timber, to keep down the cost of the temporary work. The centre should be simply constructed and kept back from the face of the arch to allow for alignment and plumbing.

8.7 Details around openings
The main consideration in the detailing of the head, jamb, and sill is the prevention of moisture penetration to the inside surfaces, since in all cases the cavity is closed. Moisture may penetrate by capillary attraction through the wall or between the wall and the window or door frame.

Head (fig. 8.13)
Water running down the face of the wall must be prevented from running back under the lintel towards the joint between lintel and frame. This is usually effected by means of a drip mould or throating.

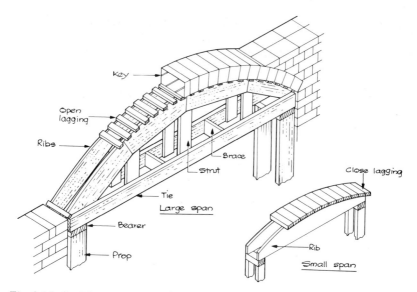

Fig. 8.12 Centring to segmental arches

Moisture is prevented from passing between the two leaves by means of a d.p.c., and this d.p.c. formed as a stepped d.p.c. also directs any moisture dropping from the cavity ties down the cavity to the outer leaf. (N.B. Weep holes should be formed in the face of the wall to allow this water to escape.)

Rain-water may bypass the throating and pass by capillary attraction between the lintel and frame, and it is therefore good practice to seal this joint externally with a mastic as well as having an anticapillary groove in the frame.

In the case of solid wall construction, as the wall is designed to operate on the sponge principle no d.p.c. is used.

Jamb (fig. 8.13)

Similar problems are encountered in the detailing of the jambs, and similar solutions are used.

In the case of a wall in an exposed situation, the joint between the frame and the head and sill may be protected by setting the frame in a rebated jamb or behind the face lintel or arch.

Sill and threshold (fig. 8.14)

The sill of a window or door projects forward of the remainder of the frame (Volume 1, Chapters 8 and 9). This feature, together with the throating, 'throws' the water running down the window or door away from the joint

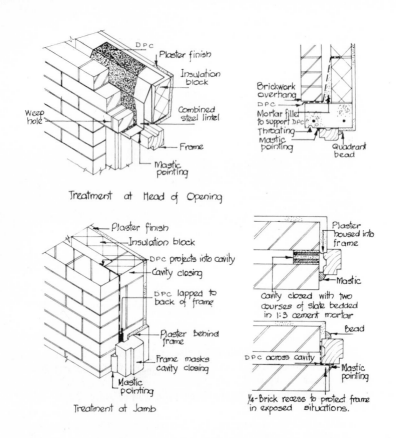

Treatment at Head of Opening

DPC
Plaster finish
Insulation block
Combined steel lintel
Weep hole
Frame
Mastic pointing

Brickwork overhang
DPC
Mortar fillet to support DPC
Throating
Mastic pointing
Quadrant bead

Treatment at Jamb

Plaster finish
Insulation block
DPC projects into cavity
Cavity closing
DPC lapped to back of frame
Plaster behind frame
Frame masks cavity closing
Mastic pointing

Plaster housed into frame
Mastic
Cavity closed with two courses of slate bedded in 1:3 cement mortar

Bead
DPC across cavity
Mastic pointing
¼-Brick recess to protect frame in exposed situations.

Fig. 8.13 Typical details at head and jamb

Cavity closing at window opening

74

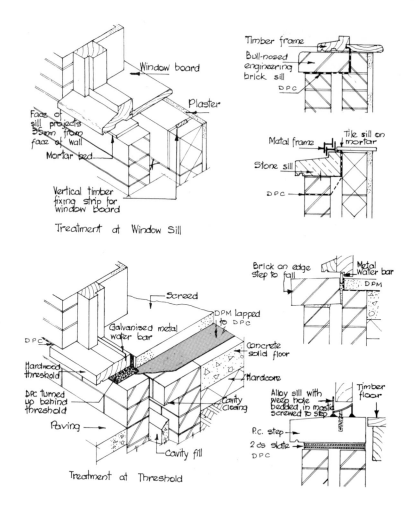

Fig. 8.14 Typical details at sill and threshold

between the sill and well. However, moisture must still be prevented from either bridging the cavity or passing to the inside surfaces, and a d.p.c. is generally the answer.

75

9   Pitched roofs

Understands the construction of timber roofs up to 7.5 m span and the application of typical coverings.

9.1 *Identifies the component parts of a roof structure and states their functions.*

9.2 *Sketches and describes typical roof forms including purlins, gables, hips and valleys.*

9.3 *Explains the principles of using trusses and trussed rafters.*

9.4 *Sketches and describes the construction and erection of timber roof trusses.*

9.5 *Identifies suitable materials for sarking and thermal insulation.*

9.6 *Identifies essential differences between double- and single-lap roof coverings.*

9.7 *Sketches and describes typical applications of the above coverings.*

Acknowledgement is due to the Technician Education Council for permission to use the content of the TEC units in this chapter. The council reserves the right to amend the content of its units at any time.

There are many types of pitched roofs and structural forms (Volume 1, Chapter 10), but the most common types in modern domestic construction are the double pitch and mono-pitch.

9.1 Roof components
The components of the roof and roof structure are as follows (fig. 9.1):

Barge-board	A sloping board at a gable, providing a neat finish to the roof.
Battens	Timber laths used as fixings for slates and tiles.
Binder	A member supporting long ceiling joists and preventing their excessive deflection.
Brace	(Also called a strut.) Provides additional support for the purlin in truss construction.
Ceiling joist	Supports the ceiling finish as well as acting as a collar.
Collar	Restrains the rafters from outward movement.
Common rafter (spar)	Inclined member set parallel to the slope of the roof covering, running from ridge to eaves and supporting the battens.

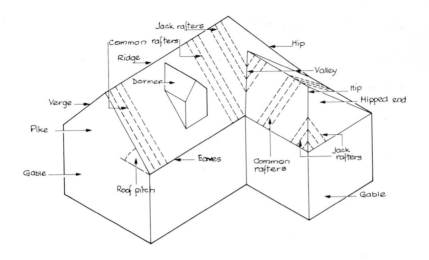

Fig. 9.1 Roof terminology

Dragon tie	A horizontal member fixed across the wall-plates at an external corner to counteract the thrust of the hip rafter.
Eaves	The lower edge of the inclined roof surface which overhangs the walls.
Fascia	A vertical board fixed to the lower end of the rafters and supporting the gutter.
Gable end	Vertical wall taken up to the ridge.
Gable	The triangular part of the gable end.
Hanger	Vertical member supporting the binder or ceiling joist from a purlin or rafter.
Hip	The line of intersection of two roof surfaces which contain an external angle greater than 180 °.
Hipped end	Triangular sloping surface formed between hips, ridge, and eaves.
Hip rafter	Forms the hip and spans from ridge to eaves.
Jack rafter	A shortened rafter spanning from eaves to hip or from ridge to valley.
King-post truss	A framework supporting the purlins with a central vertical post from ridge to collar.
Pike	See 'Gable'.
Purlin	A horizontal member supporting the rafters.
Rafter	See 'Common rafter'.

77

Ridge	The highest line of the roof; the terminations of the inclined surfaces at the top of the slope.
Ridge board	A vertical board through which the rafters are nailed to each other.
Sarking (felt)	Also known as roofing felt — laid over the rafters to keep out wind and dust.
Soffit board	A horizontal board fixed under the rafters and forming part of the eaves.
Spar	See 'Common rafter'.
Strut	See 'Brace'.
Tilting fillet	Triangular member which sets the first row of tiles at the correct angle.
Truss	A structural framework supporting the roof coverings.
Valley	The line of intersection of two roof surfaces which contain an external angle of less than 180°.
Valley rafter	Forms the valley and spans from ridge to eaves.
Verge	The overhanging edge of the covering at a gable.
Wall-plate	A generally horizontal member resting on the top of the external wall to provide a fixing for the trusses and rafters and distribute the load evenly from them to the wall.

Flush verge

9.2 Roof forms

Purlins (fig. 9.2)

The Building Regulations, approved document A, indicate that the maximum size of rafter is 50 mm x 150 mm, giving a maximum permissible span of 4.95 m (Table B15). This distance is frequently insufficient for a double- pitch domestic roof, therefore the span of the rafter must be reduced or its size increased. Any rafter size greater than 50 mm x 125 mm is not economical; thus some way must be found to reduce the span. Another support member — the purlin — placed approximately mid-way between the ridge and wall-plate will reduce the span. In the case of a gable roof, the

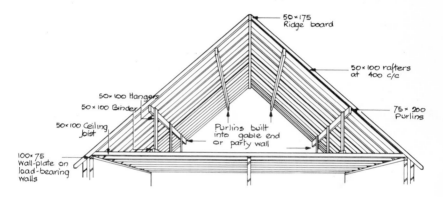

Fig. 9.2 Purlin roof

Purlin-roof construction with dormer framing

79

purlin is built into the gables or supported on corbels. In a hipped roof, the purlin forms a ring beam which is supported on pillars projecting up from internal walls or on struts bearing on load-bearing walls or ceiling joists.

Gables (fig. 9.3)
The roof may finish flush with a gable or it may project a short distance over the wall. In the latter case, the projecting verge, consisting of barge-board, soffit board, and sometimes an outer rafter, is supported by cantilever rafters which rest on the gable wall and are supported by the end rafter and the wall.

Ridge, eaves, hip, and valley details are shown in figs 9.4 to 9.7.

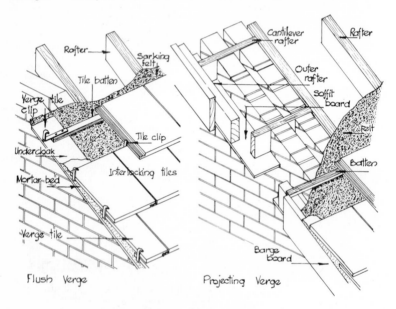

Fig. 9.3 Typical gable details

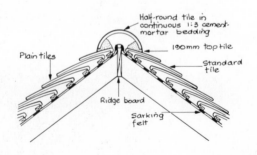

Fig. 9.4 Typical ridge details

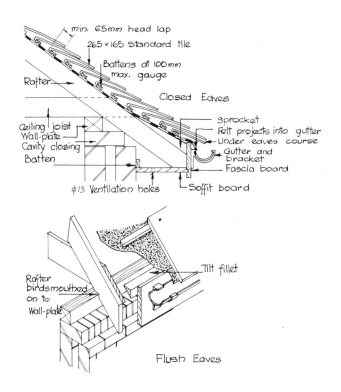

min. 65mm head lap
265×165 Standard tile
Battens at 100mm max. gauge
Rafter
Closed Eaves
Ceiling joist
Wall-plate
Cavity closing
Batten
ϕ13 Ventilation holes
Sprocket
Felt projects into gutter
Under eaves course
Gutter and bracket
Fascia board
Soffit board

Rafter birdsmouthed on to Wall-plate
Tilt fillet
Flush Eaves

Fig. 9.5 Typical eaves details

Eaves construction

81

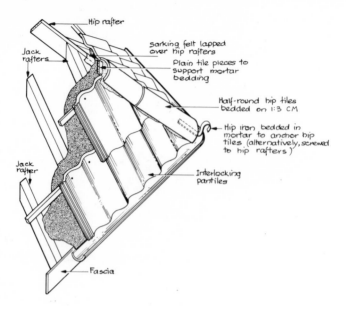

Fig. 9.6 Typical hip details

9.3 Trusses and trussed rafters

Trusses

A truss is a structural member which carries the load of a number of adjacent rafters via the purlins. As it carries more load than the normal roof members, it must have stronger members and connections. The Timber Research and Development Association (TRADA) have produced standard designs for various roof slopes or pitches and various spans (fig. 9.8). The joints between members in a truss are either lapped or gusseted, the joint being completed by nails for lightly loaded sections or by bolts used in conjunction with toothed-plate or shearing connectors for heavily loaded sections.

Trussed rafters

With the increasing costs of timber and labour over the last few years, more economic methods of roof construction have been devised. Use of the trussed rafter is the most popular and links admirably with other constructional developments such as the cross wall.

   Material of light cross-section jointed with gussets, pierced, or more commonly toothed-plate connectors is formed into trusses which are positioned at the same centres as the rafters (fig. 9.9). Their construction gives a strong load-bearing member with the main tie acting as the ceiling joist. The trusses can be designed for individual situations by a computer, which will also prepare cutting lists for the individual members and size the

82

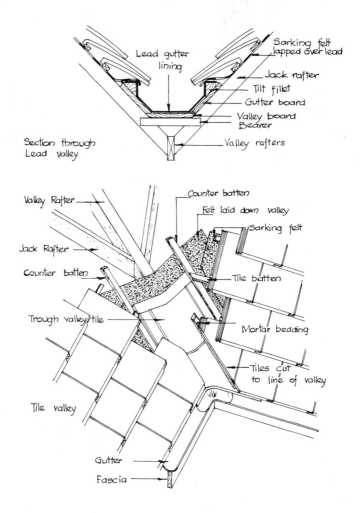

Section through Lead valley

Lead gutter lining
Sarking felt lapped over lead
Jack rafter
Tilt fillet
Gutter board
Valley board Bearer
Valley rafters

Valley Rafter
Counter batten
Felt laid down valley
Sarking felt
Jack Rafter
Counter batten
Tile batten
Trough valley tile
Mortar bedding
Tiles cut to line of valley
Tile valley
Gutter
Fascia

Fig. 9.7 Typical valley details

connections in less than a minute. With modern factory-production methods, a truss can be produced in less than five minutes; hence large savings have already been made in time and material and more are made on site.

Both the truss and the trussed rafter, like the pitched roof, are based on the triangle, which is the most rigid structural form. This triangulation provides the strength across the span, but there still remains the problem of stability along the span. Stability is provided by the purlins and ridge in the case of the truss and by the battens and runners (members similar to the binder but not intended to carry any vertical load) in the case of the trussed rafter.

83

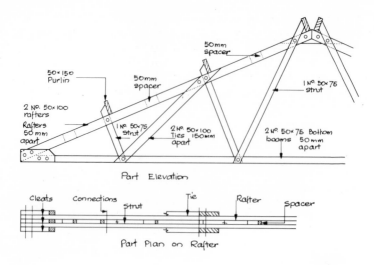

Part Elevation

Part Plan on Rafter

Fig. 9.8 Truss details

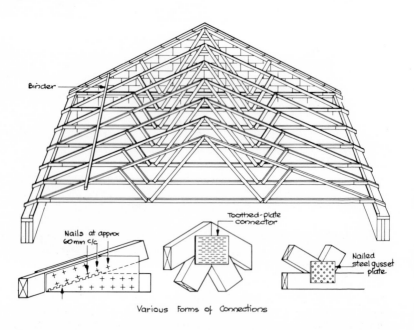

Various Forms of Connections

Fig. 9.9 Trussed-rafter details

An added advantage of these members is that the only load-bearing walls required are the external walls. However, they also have the disadvantage that the loft space is restricted, making it a more difficult operation to carry out any loft-conversion work.

9.4 Truss construction

Members of trusses may be butt-jointed or single- or double-lap-jointed (fig. 9.10). Butt joints or double-lap joints are preferred, since no eccentric loading occurs. Butt joints are made by butting the two members together and covering the joint with one or preferably two gussets or plate connectors. The gussets are usually of plywood, while the toothed plate is the most popular connector.

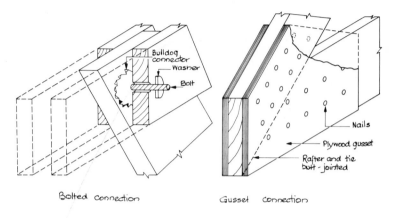

Fig. 9.10 Truss joints

In the case of the truss, as it is carrying a larger roof area than a rafter or trussed rafter, the strength of the member is nowadays generally derived from the use of two or more small-section members parallel to one another, rather than from the older construction of large solid members. The compression members in the truss are blocked together to restrict any buckling action which may occur as a result of the slenderness of the individual members.

Erection of a truss requires the use of lifting tackle or a large labour force, whereas two men can lift and position a trussed rafter on a two-storey domestic dwelling without too much difficulty.

When the trusses or rafters have been lifted into the roof area, they must be positioned and held in place. A truss is positioned at each end of a roof or length of purlin and is braced to a gable wall or other support while the purlins and ridge board are fixed in position running between the two trusses. Further trusses are initially placed horizontally across the roof span and then turned up through 90° to the vertical and attached to the purlins. Finally, the ordinary rafters are fixed to the ridge-board purlins and wall-plate (fig. 9.11).

The trussed rafters are positioned in a similar manner but are held in position by short lengths of batten tacked between two adjacent members.

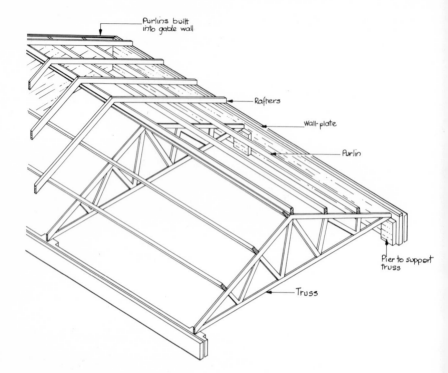

Fig. 9.11 Truss construction

When a number of these trussed rafters are positioned, the runners are permanently fixed. The temporary battening is removed when the permanent tile battens are fixed.

In order to prevent the whole of a roof being lifted off the building as a result of wind suction, it is common practice to anchor the wall-plate to the wall by means of galvanised metal straps (fig. 9.12). These straps are built into the inner leaf of the cavity wall some six courses below eaves level, run up the cavity, bent over, and fixed to the top of the wall-plate.

9.5 Sarking and thermal insulation
The Building Regulations (part C, clause C4) require that 'the walls, floors and roof of the building shall adequately resist the passage of moisture to the inside of the building.'

Part L of the Building Regulations (clause L2) requires the thermal transmittance (U–value) of a domestic roof to be not greater than 0.35 W/m^2 $^\circ$C, and 0.7 W/m^2 $^\circ$C for an industrial building. Table 3 in approved document L gives thicknesses of insulating materials and constructional modifiers which will meet the requirements. Typical constructions are shown in fig. 9.13.

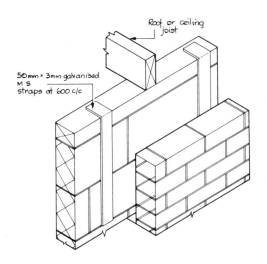

Fig. 9.12 Wall-plate anchorage

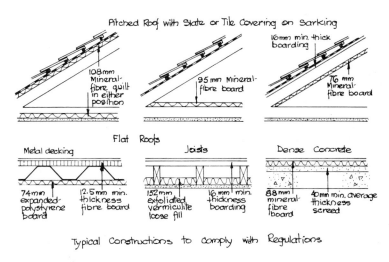

Fig. 9.13 Roof insulation

Moisture is generally prevented from entering the building by the roof covering, but driven snow and rain may find its way past the main covering, and for this reason sarking felt provides an additional barrier element. There are a number of types of roofing felt which may be used (**BS 747:1977**) but, since the felt will be punctured by nails when the tile battens are fixed, the untearable varieties (i.e. those on a woven base) are preferred. Unless the felt is supported on boarding, it will sag between the rafters since it is laid parallel

87

to the ridge with 150 mm laps between sheets. This sag allows any moisture bypassing the roof covering to run down to the eaves, where it is discharged into the guttering.

The insulation may be provided under the roof covering or above the ceiling. Under the covering, a sarking felt with aluminium-foil backing will improve the insulation, used together with woodwool slabs, corkboard, mineral fibre in either quilt, board, or rigid-slab form, or expanded poly-styrene boards. However, for normal domestic construction it is more usual to lay mineral-fibre quilt, mat, or pelletted loose fill (60 mm minimum thickness), or exfoliated vermiculite loose fill (70 mm minimum thickness) in direct contact with the ceiling (i.e. between the ceiling joists).

9.6 Coverings
The essential difference between single-lap and double-lap roof coverings is that the single-lap coverings interlock whereas the double-lap coverings do not.

Double-lap coverings (fig. 9.14)
These comprise slates, stone slates, plain tiles, and shingles. With the excep-tion of the plain tiles, which are slightly cambered and have nibs on one end, they are flat units and are laid by butt jointing one tile to the next along the roof. Moisture is prevented from entering the roof space by ensuring that there are at least two thicknesses of tile covering any part of the roof. This is done by overlapping one course of tiles by another and staggering the position of the butt joints. The pitch of the roof is also critical in preventing moisture being driven under the overlap by wind, and, in the case of tiles, capillary attraction is prevented by the camber of the tile.

Single-lap coverings (fig. 9.15)
For domestic construction these are mainly concrete or clay tiles which have preformed interlocking grooves. These grooves overcome the problems of moisture penetration both at the sides and at the bottom of the tile. Alter-

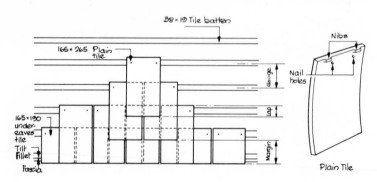

Fig. 9.14 Double-lap terminology

88

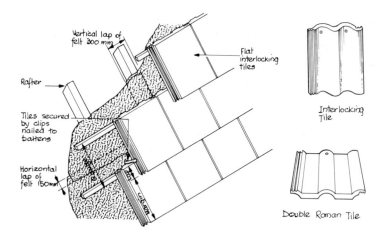

Fig. 9.15 Single-lap terminology

natives are the curved 'pantile' or the 'double roman tile', both of which use their curved surfaces to provide the overlap.

In the majority of cases these coverings can be laid on roofs having a much lower pitch than is required for the double-lap coverings.

9.7 Covering details (fig. 9.16)
There are several standard fittings which are available with the majority of the roof coverings and take care of difficult situations such as valleys, hips,

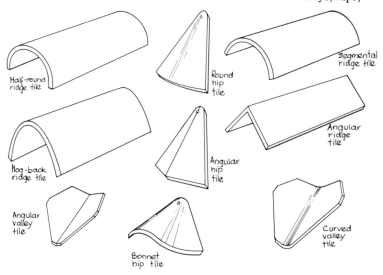

Fig. 9.16 Special tile shapes

ridges, and verges. These, together with their minimum quality standards, are covered by British Standards.

Double-lap coverings

It is essential that the fixing of the covering remains intact for many years. The fixing is provided by galvanised nails driven into the battens through pre-formed holes in the slates or tiles. The nails are generally protected by two thicknesses of covering, but, in the case of centre-nailed covering only one thickness of covering is provided.

The key factor in any roof-covering operation is the positioning (gauge) of the tile battens to receive the fixing. This is determined by the size of the covering unit (slate or tile), the siting of the fixing hole, and the amount of lap required:

$$\text{head-nailed gauge (mm)} = \frac{\text{length of slate (mm)} - (\text{lap} + 25)\text{ mm}}{2}$$

$$\text{centre-nailed gauge (mm)} = \frac{\text{length of slate (mm)} - \text{lap (mm)}}{2}$$

Ridge tiles and hip tiles (with the exception of the bonnet tile) have no holes for fixing and are held in place by the adhesive effect of their mortar bed. To prevent the hip tiles sliding down the roof, a hip hook is frequently screwed to the top of the hip rafter at its lower end.

Besides the use of special tiles etc. at hips and valleys, sheet lead can also be used to form a weather seal at these points, provided that it is adequately supported.

At the eaves and ridge, in order to maintain the double thickness, a cut tile or slate is used.

Valley construction

Single-lap coverings

Similar construction details to those for the double-lap apply to these coverings. The nibs on the back of the tiles (also on the plain tile) form an anchorage for the tile on the batten and, as a result, depending on the degree of exposure of the roof to the wind, there is no necessity to nail down every tile — indeed, some firms recommend that only every third course is nailed, with the exception of those tiles at the eaves, at a verge, or next to a valley or hip, since the self weight of a tile plus the weight of the one over-lapping it will provide adequate anchorage.

Where a pitched roof abuts a wall, moisture is prevented from penetrating the surface by means of flashing and soakers (fig. 9.17). Made by a plumber from sheet lead, the soaker fits on top of the tile (in the case of single-lap coverings) or underneath the tile (in the case of double-lap coverings) and is turned up the wall; the flashing is slotted into the mortar joints of the wall and is turned down over the soaker. This prevents moisture running down or against the wall penetrating the roof surface, while allowing thermal and structural movement to take place. In order to reduce the amount of lead used, the flashing is stepped.

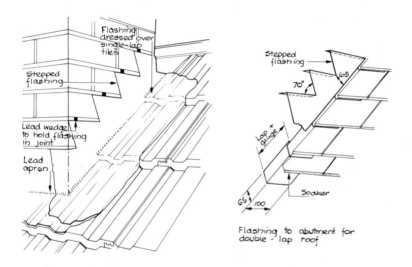

Fig. 9.17 Flashings and soakers

91

10   Flat roofs

Understands the construction of timber-joisted flat roofs up to 4.000 m span.

10.1   *Identifies component parts of a flat roof structure and states their functions.*
10.2   *Describes mastic-asphalt and built-up-felt roof finishes.*
10.3   *Identifies suitable materials for boarding, thermal insulation and vapour barriers.*
10.4   *Sketches and describes the construction of a timber-joisted flat roof including details at eaves, verges, and abutments.*
10.5   *Sketches and describes sheet-metal roofing.*

Acknowledgement is due to the Technician Education Council for permission to use the content of the TEC units in this chapter. The council reserves the right to amend the content of its units at any time.

10.1 Components

The component parts of a timber flat roof structure are

Roof joists	Span from wall to wall, providing the structural support. Guidance to their size and span is given in Tables B21 to B24 in approved document A of the Building Regulations.
Firrings (firring pieces)	Tapered wooden pieces fixed to the joists to provide falls on the finished roof (fig. 10.1).
Decking, boarding	Rough boards or rigid sheet material laid on the firrings to provide the support to the coverings.
Vapour barrier	A sheet membrane preventing the passage of water vapour through the decking, which would cause blistering of the asphalt or felt surface. Condensation of the vapour will also reduce the value of any insulation material in the roof space.

10.2 Coverings

Mastic asphalt (figs 10.2 and 10.3)
Mastic asphalt is a combination of asphaltic cement and mineral aggregate. The asphaltic cement is a mixture of bitumen or lake asphalt with an oil which makes the bitumen less viscous and also improves its adhesive qualities.

92

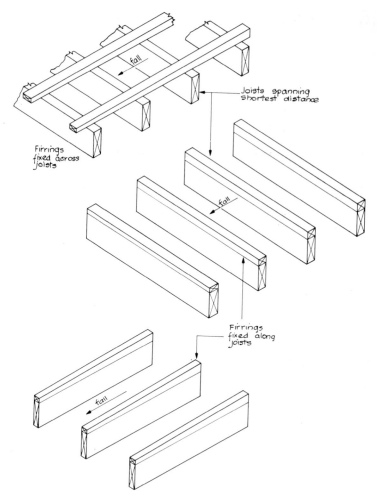

Fig. 10.1 Firrings

The mineral aggregate is either natural rock or limestone. There are two British Standards for mastic asphalt — BS 6577:1985 for that containing natural rock aggregate and **BS** 988:1973 for that containing limestone aggregate. The former material tends to have a greyish colour when weathered, while the latter remains dark. Both types of mastic asphalt harden and shrink in direct sunlight, causing crazing, and they are usually covered with a reflective layer such as a 12 mm thickness of limestone chippings or other light-coloured rock material.

Asphalt can tolerate slow movement, but rapid changes such as those resulting from thermal expansion and contraction will cause cracking. Because of the material's high coefficient of thermal expansion, it should

93

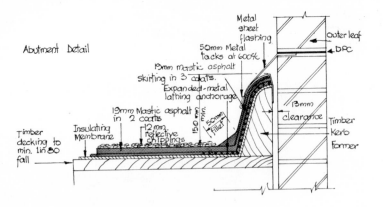

Fig. 10.2 Mastic-asphalt details

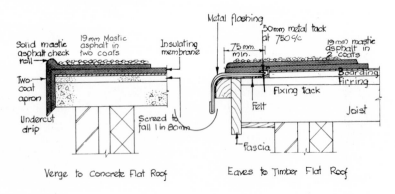

Verge to Concrete Flat Roof   Eaves to Timber Flat Roof

Fig. 10.3 Mastic-asphalt details

be separated from the supporting structure, and special care should be taken in detailing at the edges of the covering. The self weight of the roof covering (40 kg/m² for a 19 mm thickness) is sufficient to prevent uplift resulting from wind suction. It is usual to lay the asphalt in two equal layers of about 10 mm thickness on a felt underlay, with falls of between 1 in 80 and 1 in 40.

Felt (figs 10.4 and 10.5)
Bitumen felts consist of bitumen strengthened and stabilised by fibres, asbestos, or glass fibre in accordance with BS 747:1977.

Three layers of felt are required on all but temporary buildings, where two layers should suffice. The first layer is nailed to the timber decking using large-headed galvanised nails – this allows a certain amount of relative movement between the covering and the decking without the problems of uplift.

94

The felt, supplied in rolls, is laid broken joint (i.e. the first layer across the slope, the second layer down the slope, the third layer again across the slope), each layer having 75 mm side laps and being bonded to the subsequent layer with hot or cold bitumen. Again the top surface of the roof finish must be protected from the effects of sunlight, either by a 12 mm covering of reflective chippings or by a felt which contains a surface coating of coloured mineral granules.

As with asphalt, the felt covering is brittle and, when it is to be bent around the edges of the roof, it should first be softened by heat prior to fixing, otherwise cracking will result. There is now available decking which has the built-up roof covering incorporated and which only requires the joints between panels to be bonded. Suitable falls for this covering vary between 1 in 60 and 1 in 40.

10.3 Subsurface materials

Boarding

Rough timber boards, tongue-and-grooved boards, chipboard, and plywood are all used for decking material and are suitable for support at 400 to 450 mm centres. The boards should be laid with the fall so that any subsequent drying shrinkage will not impede the flow of water off the roof. The sheet materials require fixing around their perimeter, and solid filling — known as noggings — will be required between the joists. The noggings may also serve the purpose of strutting between the joists (see suspended timber floors, Volume 1, Chapter 13). The nails in all cases should be well punched home.

Protection from fungal decay should be given to all timbers (N.B. avoid creosote when using felt roofing), and in certain areas near the River Thames (identified in Table 1 of the approved document supporting Regulation 7) all softwood roofing timber, including ceiling joists in the roof space, should be adequately treated against house-longhorn-beetle infestation.

Other alternatives to the timber decking materials include woodwool and compressed-strawboard slabs. The woodwool slabs, 50 mm thick, require a 12 mm sand—cement screed on their upper surface, as well as the joints between slabs being made with mortar. These slabs will span 600 mm, therefore the joist centres can be increased provided the joists are designed for the increased loading. For small roof spans, the joists may be dispensed with completely if the long edges of the woodwool slabs are reinforced with metal channelling. The woodwool also has the advantage of providing a certain amount of thermal insulation to the roof structure.

Compressed strawboard also provides insulation and in a 50 mm thickness will also span 600 mm. All edges of the slabs must be fully supported and all joints taped with strips of roofing felt bonded to the slab with bitumen. The slabs should never be left exposed to the weather and should have adequate ventilation at all times.

Thermal insulation

It has already been stated that compressed-strawboard and woodwool slabs provide a degree of insulation; this can be improved by laying mineral-fibre, vegetable fibre, or granular boards or a lightweight aggregate screed on top of these slabs. However, with a joisted structure the mineral-fibre quilt is still the most popular material and the easiest to insert.

Vapour barrier

This membrane should be situated on the warmer side of the insulation material, in order to prevent condensation occurring within the insulation. This generally means immediately between the ceiling and the joists. The most convenient method of providing the barrier is by a layer of aluminium foil, especially when many types of board can be obtained with a foil backing already incorporated. The foil may also be incorporated in a form of roofing felt, when it is covered both sides with bitumen strengthened with glass fibre.

10.4 Covering details

Eaves

In order to form a drip for the water to fall into a gutter, the felt is either trimmed into and over a preformed metal section (usually aluminium) or is turned up under itself and fixed to a fillet which, in turn, is fixed to the fascia (fig. 10.4).

The asphalt is usually finished on top of a metal trim or drip.

Felt roofing

96

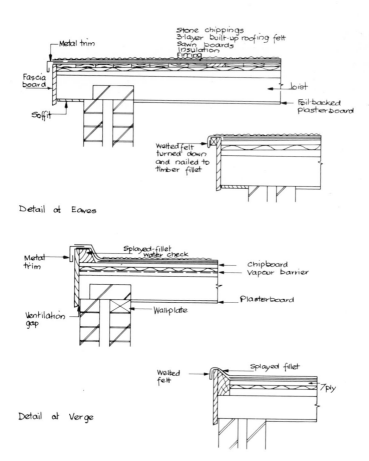

Fig. 10.4 Felt-roof details

Verge

The edge of the roof at the verge usually has an upstand which directs the water away from the roof edge and down to the eaves. The top two layers of the roofing felt are taken over the timber former, and the finish is again by metal trim, by turned-down drip, or by a separate strip of felt forming the drip and being bonded over the roof felt down the former and on to the flat roof surface for some 75 mm (fig. 10.4). The asphalt covering is also finished by metal trim (fig. 10.2).

Abutment

The problems of moisture penetration where a flat roof abuts a wall are similar to those of the pitched roof. The solution is similar except that, since the coverings are 'flexible', the material is turned up the wall, i.e. forming a composite soaker. For the felt roof, the top two layers can be turned 150 mm up the wall or separate felt soakers can be used. The flashing is usually lead but, in the case of a low parapet, felt may be used to form a continuous flashing/soaker. To prevent a sharp upturn of felt at the junction of the roof and wall, which would cause the felt to crack after a period of time, due to thermal movement, a timber former is used to ease the felt around the angle (fig. 10.5).

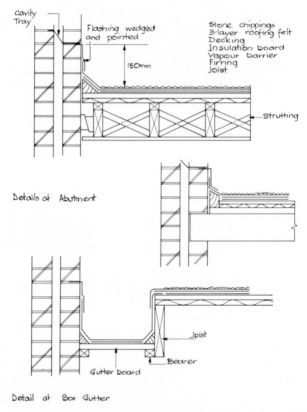

Fig. 10.5 Felt-roof details

The asphalt covering may also be eased around the angle or be reinforced by a two-coat fillet. All vertical work, known as skirting, is done in three coats as opposed to two coats on the flat, and the asphalt upstand is flashed over by a metal flashing (fig. 10.3).

On a roof surrounded by parapet walls, a drainage hole is formed in one of the walls and the asphalt covering and skirting are run through the opening and lapped on to a metal spitter which discharges the rain-water into a rain-water hopper.

10.5 Sheet-metal roofing (fig. 10.6)

The older timber flat roofs were covered with sheet-metal coverings, usually of lead, copper, or zinc. However, because of their weight, the length of a roll of these materials is much less than the roll length of roofing felt, and more frequent jointing is required. The covering consists of a single skin of the sheet material, and therefore no fixing can be made through the sheet, the self weight of the material providing the majority of the fixing. The detailing at the joints must therefore provide a fixing while remaining water-tight and at the same time allowing thermal expansion to take place. Details at abutments are similar to those for felt or asphalt, but without a former. Joints which run parallel to the fall are constructed using a wooden *roll* former and occur at approximately 600 to 800 mm centres.

The length of any sheet down the slope should not exceed 2.5 m for lead or 3.0 m for copper. The joint resulting from this limitation in lead roofing is called a *drip* and requires a step in the roof surface (fig. 10.7). It is there-

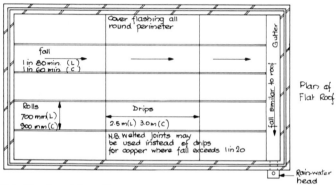

Fig. 10.6 Sheet-metal roofing

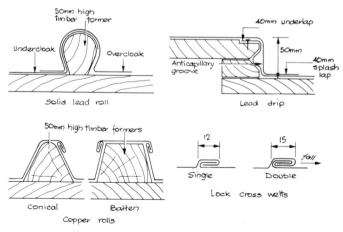

Fig. 10.7 Drips and rolls

99

fore easier to construct the structural support with the joists running across the fall rather than parallel to it. Copper sheets may be jointed using the similar technique of the drip, or welted joints may be used.

The thickness of these coverings will depend on the anticipated traffic across them, but common lead thicknesses are 1.8 mm and 2.2 mm (codes 4 and 5 in BS 1178:1982 and in accordance with CP 143:part 11:1970), while copper thicknesses of 0.6 mm and 0.7 mm are commonly used (BS 2870:1980 and CP 143:part 12:1970). The falls for these metal roof coverings should not be less than 1 in 80 for lead and 1 in 60 for copper.

On a roof surrounded by parapets, a gutter is constructed to gather the water at one discharge point (fig. 10.8).

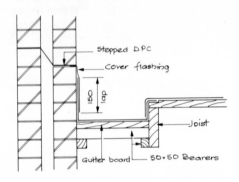

Fig. 10.8 Gutter construction

11   Windows

Understands the main factors affecting choice of windows and draws typical details.

11.1   Identifies main factors affecting choice of window type.
11.2   Prepares window schedule including ironmongery from drawing and trade literature.
11.3   Sketches and describes typical window details at head, sill and jamb including fixings and provision for finishings.
11.4   Identifies main types of glass and methods of glazing.

Acknowledgement is due to the Technician Education Council for permission to use the content of the TEC units in this chapter. The council reserves the right to amend the content of its units at any time.

11.1 Selection of windows
The main factors affecting the choice of a window type are:
a) *Cost*   Purpose-made items are far more expensive than standard units produced in bulk by the manufacturer.
b) *Availability*   Certain types of window, although standard, may have a long delivery period.
c) *Appearance*   The type of window will affect the appearance not only of the window but also of the property.
d) *Light*   The amount of natural light required in a given room will determine the minimum size of window.
e) *Ventilation*   The amount of ventilation required will determine the number and size of opening lights.
f) *Maintenance*   The ease with which a window may be maintained is a further consideration. The amount of painting, or the lack of it in the case of aluminium frames, is a major factor, especially in large office blocks.

11.2 Scheduling
In order that a contractor may understand the architect's wishes regarding window type and fittings, a schedule is prepared showing in tabular form the exact requirements for a window in a given location and property.

The schedule shown in fig. 11.1 will have been taken off a set of plans. Should the layout be handed, those windows indicated as being handed on the schedule will be standard, and vice versa. Other information, such as the details of the ironmongery required for a particular window, may also be included.

WINDOW SCHEDULE
FOR
HOUSE TYPE B3

Window	Type	Handing	Glazing	Lintel	Window Board	Ironmongery
W1	440 Tx	As catalogue	4mm OQ 5mm OQ	CNP 4c	150 × 25 SW	As supplied with frame
W2	340 TW	—"—	as W1	CNP 4a	Glazed tile	—"—
W3	340 PWV	opposite to catalogue	as W1	CNP 4a	150 × 25 SW	—"—
W4	140 V	As catalogue	as W1	CN 1	—'—	—"—
W5	N 36 V	—"—	4mm obscured	CN 1	—"—	—•—
W6	436 TW	—"—	as W5	CNP 6/6c	—"—	—"—
W7	336 TW	opposite to catalogue	as W1	CNP 6/6a	—"—	—•—
W8	236 V	—•r—	as W1	CNP 5/6a	—"—	—"—
W9	3036 WV	As catalogue	4mm & 5mm obscured	CNP 3	Glazed tile	—"—
W10	136 V	—"—	as W5	CNP 5/6a	—•—	—"—
W11	136 V	—"—	as W1	CNP 3	150 × 25 SW	—•—

Fig. 11.1 Typical window schedule

11.3 Installation

Typical details of timber and metal windows have already been shown in
Volume 1 (Chapter 8) and the inclusion of windows in a building was
partially discussed in section 8.7.

Timber windows may be fixed into the envelope either during the
construction of the walls or afterwards. Where the window is fixed during
construction, galvanised metal fishtail ties may be fixed to the jambs and
built into the mortar joints of the wall. It is more usual to fit the frame after
the wall has been built, so that no vertical loading is imposed on the frame.
In this case, treated timber pallets or plugs are built into the mortar joints at
the jamb, and the window frame is screwed or nailed to them. Timber frames
are seldom fixed at the head or sill.

The internal finishes generally consist of plaster to the head and jambs
(occasionally a timber lining in older construction) and a window board or
tiles to the sill. In order to prevent gaps appearing between the finish and
the frame, as a result of structural or thermal movement, the joint is usually
masked. This masking is achieved by running the plaster or lining into a
rebate formed in the frame, or by covering the joint between the two with
a cover bead. Besides being supported by a groove in the sill of the window
frame, the window board is also supported on timber pallets driven into the
vertical joints at the top of the inner leaf. The window board projects into

the room, over the plaster finish to the wall underneath, thereby protecting and masking the joint (figs 8.13 and 8.14).

Metal windows may be fixed using metal lugs driven into or bedded in the joints of the wall, or be screwed to timber plugs as in the case of timber window frames. In these two cases the frame is bedded in a waterproof cement–sand mortar. The metal frame may also be fixed inside a timber frame, in which case the detailing of the rebates in the timber frame is amended, or the metal frame may be located on a timber strip previously located on the wall jambs (fig. 11.2).

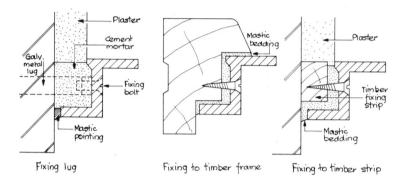

Fixing lug   Fixing to timber frame   Fixing to timber strip

Fig. 11.2 Metal-window fixing

11.4 Glass and glazing

There are many types of glass available for a vast range of situations. Glass consists of silica, cullet or broken glass, alumina, calcium carbonate, and other materials in small quantities for specific effects. The materials, inserted in a furnace, fuse together at approximately 1500 °C.

The sheet glass is formed by drawing, rolling, or floating.

a) *Drawn glass*   The glass is drawn vertically upwards from the molten mixture through rollers and, as it cools, is cut to size and stored. This method is used to produce most of the clear sheet glass used for glazing purposes, in a range of thicknesses varying between 2 mm and 6 mm (2 mm is unsuitable for general glazing).

b) *Rolled glass*   Drawn horizontally through rollers, the glass is annealed before it is cut and stored. The rollers may be embossed, in which case obscured or patterned glass is obtained. This process is also used to produce ground, smoothed, or polished glass which is free from distortion.

c) *Float glass*   The molten glass is floated across a bed of liquid tin before being cooled and annealed. By careful control of temperature, a transparent plate glass is produced which is perfectly flat and free from distortion, in a range of thicknesses from 3 to 12 mm.

BS 952: part 1:1978 lists a number of different types of glass and glazing qualities.

a) *Transparent*   This type of glass transmits a high percentage of light (approx. 85%) and permits clear vision. There are various qualities:

  i) horticultural — inferior quality

  ii) OQ (ordinary quality) — for general work

  iii) SQ (selected quality) — for better-class work

  iv) SSQ (special selected quality) — for high-grade work such as cabinets

    A 3 mm thickness is generally used, but for pane sizes exceeding 1 m^2 a 4 mm thickness should be used, and over 2 m^2 a 5 mm thickness would be required.

b) *Clear plate*   This is produced by grinding and polishing or by the float process and gives undistorted vision. It is supplied in three qualities:

  i) GG (general glazing)

  ii) SG (selected glazing) — suitable for mirrors

  iii) SQ (silvering quality) — for high-grade mirrors

c) *Translucent*   This gives diffused light. There are many patterns, including rough-cast and rolled (only one side textured), fluted, ribbed, reeded, cathedral, hammered, etc.

d) *Wired*   A wire mesh embedded in the glass holds it together on fracture. In the Georgian wired, the glass is rough cast and contains a 12 mm-square wire mesh, while the hexagonal-wired contains a 20 mm hexagonal mesh.

    The above are just a few of the types of glass available — many more are made to suit specialist situations, such as heat-resistant glass and safety glass.

Glazing (fig. 11.3)

This is the fixing of the glass in the framework. Generally the glass should have a 2 mm clearance all round the frame into which it is being fitted, in order to accommodate thermal movement. There are four basic methods.

a) *Glazing compounds*   The glass is bedded into the compound set in the rebate of the frame, thus ensuring an even seating for the glass. The glass is held in position in the frame by sprigs (for timber frames) and spring clips (for metal frames). Front putty/compound is built up to a suitable angle, but care should be taken to see that the sight lines from the window are not obstructed.

    There are two groups of glazing compounds:

  i) those requiring maintenance and protection, such as linseed-oil putty (for timber frames), metal-casement putty (for metal frames), and flexible compounds;

  ii) those not requiring protection, such as non-setting compounds, sealants, synthetic-rubber gaskets, and plastics strips.

b) *Beading*   Similar to (a) but the glass, set in a glazing compound, is held in position by a timber or metal beading fixed to the frame by nails or screws. In order to maintain a weather seal on external windows, the beading should also be set in compound. For glazing in internal doors, a wash-leather strip may be used in place of the glazing compound, the wash leather absorbing the shock of a door being slammed or jarred.

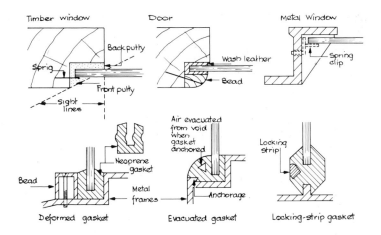

Fig. 11.3 Glazing

c) *Gaskets*   This method depends on the gasket being compressed against
the glass both to form a watertight seal and to grip the glass and hold it in
position. The gasket is manufactured in one piece from resilient material
such as neoprene, and the tensioning is achieved by inserting a zipper
strip into the gasket.

d) *Gasket and bead*   A combination of (b) and (c), the gasket being
anchored by beading.

12 Concrete slabs

Understands the construction of simply supported r.c. slabs.

12.1 Sketches and describes the construction of a simply supported in-situ r.c. slab including sequence of operations and location and purpose of reinforcement.

12.2 Explains the functions of screeds.

12.3 Describes materials used and methods of applying screeds.

Acknowledgement is due to the Technician Education Council for permission to use the content of the TEC units in this chapter. The council reserves the right to amend the content of its units at any time.

In many instances of suspended-floor construction, timber would be unsuitable because of span, deflection, floor-space size, rigidity, and wear. Reinforced concrete generally provides the alternative form of construction.

12.1 The concrete floor slab

Floors may span in one, two, or three directions, as may roofs (Volume 1, Chapter 10). The suspended-timber floor spans in two directions — the joists spanning in one direction and the floor boards spanning across them. The simple concrete floor slab may span in one or two directions depending on the support available, the support usually being provided by load-bearing walls.

The simply supported in-situ concrete slab will require soffit support during the casting operation and subsequent period, until it has gained sufficient strength. This soffit support is provided by formwork in one of two ways (see figs 7.4 and 12.1):

a) a framework of adjustable props supports horizontal ledgers which in turn support joists and the plywood decking;

b) adjustable metal joists support the decking and bear on ledgers adjacent to the perimeter walls, the ledgers again being supported by adjustable props. The metal joists are precambered so that, when the in-situ concrete is placed, the load imposed will flatten the joist. This method can reduce the number of props required under the decking to maintain a level soffit.

In order to prevent any instability in the temporary support work, the props should be braced, having first been adjusted to the correct heights by levelling the decking.

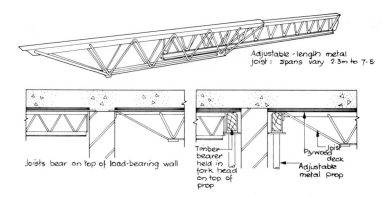

Adjustable-length metal joist: spans vary 2.3m to 7.5

Joists bear on top of load-bearing wall

Timber bearer held in fork head on top of prop

Plywood deck

Joist deck

Adjustable metal prop

Fig. 12.1 Decking formwork

The formwork to the sides of the slab is fixed to the supporting wall, the bearers being held by tie wires and wedges or by nails fixed through the bearer into the wall by a cartridge tool (fig. 12.2).

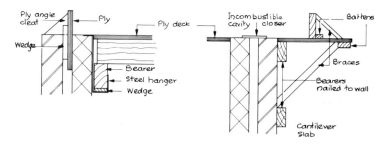

Ply angle cleat

Ply

Ply deck

Incombustible cavity | closer

Battens

Wedge

Bearer

Steel hanger

Wedge

Braces

Bearers nailed to wall

Cantilever Slab

Fig. 12.2 Edge forms

Joints formed in the slab for any reason are constructed in a similar manner to the daywork joint discussed in section 5.7(c).

The student should by now be aware that concrete is weak in tension and is reinforced by steel bars or mesh to provide additional tensile strength. A simply supported slab will sag under load and, as a result, tension is created in the section near the soffit; thus reinforcement is placed in this region. However, simple supports do not occur in actual construction — the support is not a knife edge but a flat wall top, and there is generally load in the form of walls above the slab at the support. These factors alter the way in which the slab bends and, as a result, the areas where tension occurs, thus requiring amendment to the positioning of the reinforcement.

The size and amount of reinforcement required in a floor slab depends mainly on the loading imposed and the depth and span of the slab. In order to spread the loading equally across the slab and relieve any highly stressed areas, distribution steel (running at right angles to the main steel) is used, being tied to the main steel by special 1 mm-gauge malleable tying wire. The steel reinforcement is again placed as close as possible to the high-stress region in the slab (i.e. the bottom or top surface), bearing in mind the amount of cover required to transmit those tensile forces from the concrete to the steel (fig. 12.3). The concrete cover to the reinforcement also provides protection from damage to the structure by fire, moisture, and corrosive agents.

The location of the steel during the concreting operation is by spacers (concrete or plastics) and stools.

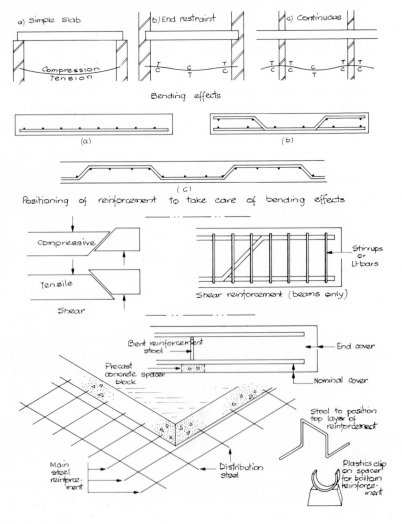

Fig. 12.3 Reinforcement to slabs

12.2 Functions of screeds

A screed is a mixture of cement and aggregate applied to the upper surface of a concrete floor or roof. It may perform one or more of the following functions.

a) *Provide a smooth surface* on which to lay a floor finish. This finish may be applied directly to the concrete slab (see section 5.6(g)) but on smaller areas it is more convenient to use a screed some 40 mm thick.

b) *Provide falls* to the surface. It is easier to create falls on the surface of a concrete slab using a semi-dry screed than it is when dealing with the wet concrete.

c) *Embed services,* such as electricity cables in conduit, hot- and cold-water pipes, central-heating pipes, and gas pipes. These are more readily accommodated or ducted in a screed than in the concrete slab.

d) *Accommodate under-floor heating cables* or pipes.

e) *Provide thermal insulation* by the use of lightweight aggregate in the screed. This is important in multi-occupancy buildings or areas where a controlled environment is required.

f) *Provide sound insulation* by constructing a floating floor. The screed being laid on a compressible layer of sound-insulating material will prevent the transmission of noise through the floor structure.

g) *Protection of a damp-proof membrane* where the membrane is positioned on top of the structure concrete slab.

h) *Provide a hard-wearing surface finish* in high-traffic areas such as entrance halls, landings, and corridors.

12.3 Screed materials and methods of application (figs 12.4 and 12.5)

The materials used for screeds are:

  ordinary Portland cement, conforming to BS 12;
  fine aggregates conforming to BS 882;
  coarse aggregates (chippings) having a maximum size of 10 mm.
  There are several methods of laying screeds.

a) Monolithic   The screed is laid on an in-situ concrete floor before that concrete has fully set (i.e. within three hours of the concrete being placed). This method is used for a granolithic finish. The dense topping — consisting of a 1:1:2 mix of cement, sand, and granite chippings — is applied in a single layer, the thickness varying between 15 and 25 mm. This surface provides good impact-, abrasion-, and slip-resistance, as well as low porosity.

b) Separate construction   Generally used where a further floor finish is to be used on top of the screed or where a terrazzo or alternative granolithic finish is to be applied.

  i) *Ordinary screeds* consist of a mix varying from 1:2 to 1:4½ of cement and sand, mixed with sufficient water to give adequate compaction. (The mix should ball together but not exude moisture when squeezed in the hand.) The concrete slab surface should be clean, rough (tamped finish

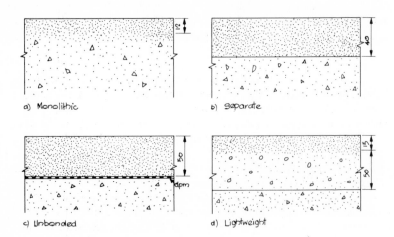

Fig. 12.4 Screed construction

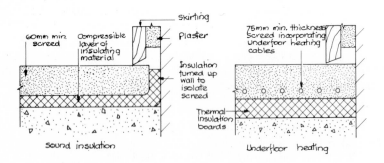

Fig. 12.5 Screed uses

or mechanically scabbled), and damp to reduce the suction of moisture from the screed into the slab. Immediately before the screed is laid, in bays, the slab surface is coated with a cement grout or other bonding agent.

Screed thicknesses vary between 30 and 75 mm. Over 40 mm thick, the screed should be laid in two layers, the top layer being thinner than the bottom one and laid immediately the lower layer has been compacted. A wood-float finish provides an open-textured surface, while a steel trowel produces a fine smooth finish.

ii) The *terrazzo* finish consists of graded crushed marble in a white or coloured cement matrix. Laid in situ, bays should not exceed 1.2 m², with brass, ebonite, or plastics strips between them. After hardening for four days, the surface is abraded and polished using a carborundum machine.

110

iii) The separate *granolithic* screed uses a similar mix and thickness to the monolithic construction but requires similar slab-surface preparation to the ordinary screed.

c) Unbonded construction   Used where the screed is laid on top of a d.p.m. or insulation layer. The minimum thickness required is 50 mm, but where heating cables or pipes are incorporated the thickness should be at least 60 mm and in the case of a floating floor 60 mm if there is no insulating layer and 75 mm where an insulating layer is incorporated.

d) Lightweight concrete screeds consist of either aerated concrete or concrete using lightweight aggregates such as vermiculite or perlite. In both cases the material is laid on a surface similar to that required for ordinary screed, to a minimum thickness of 50 mm, and lightly tamped. A dense topping of 1:3 cement—sand screed 15 to 20 mm thick is then laid on the surface within three hours, so that monolithic construction is achieved. The topping is required because the lightweight screed is weak and would be unable to carry any loadings imposed on it.

All screeds should be protected from damage until a curing period of at least a week has elapsed, and in the case of ordinary screeds receiving a further surface this protection should be provided until the final surface is applied. Curing of the screed is carried out by covering the surface with waterproof sheets, thereby reducing the speed of drying out and the likelihood of shrinkage cracking.

13   Stud partitions

Understands the construction of stud partitions.

13.1   Sketches and describes the construction of stud partitions including various finishes, fixings and details around openings.

Acknowledgement is due to the Technician Education Council for permission to use the content of the TEC units in this chapter. The council reserves the right to amend the content of its units at any time.

Stud partitions consist of a timber framework supporting a dry lining material such as plasterboard, plywood, or hardboard. They form a lightweight partition which is essentially non-load-bearing. It must be capable of supporting its own weight and resisting impact loadings from doors closing or from people and furniture banging into the surface. This form of internal wall is much quicker to erect than the traditional wet brick or block wall and is also much lighter in weight.

The timber framework consists of a sole-plate, studs, a head or head-plate, and noggings (fig. 13.1). The sole-plate rests on and is fixed to the floor construction. In the case of a ground-floor slab, it is usual to rest the sole-plates on lengths of damp-proof course irrespective of where the d.p.m. is positioned.

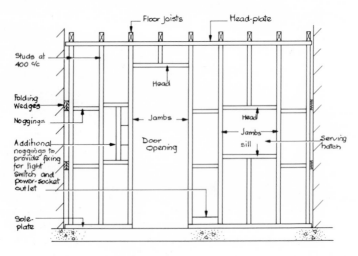

Fig. 13.1 Partition terminology

The head-plate is fixed vertically above the sole-plate to the ceiling, and the studs (vertical members) span at intervals between head- and sole-plates and are commonly skew-nailed to them. The positioning of the studs depends on the size of the lining material, but, since most of these linings have a standard sheet size of 2.4 m x 1.2 m, the studs can be conveniently set at 400 mm centres.

Since the studs form long columns, they are not very stable and, in order to increase this stability, as well as the rigidity of the whole framework, noggings are fixed across the space between the studs. Depending on the lining material, there may be one, two, or three sets of noggings in a frame. They are fixed in a similar manner to that used for solid strutting in suspended-timber-floor construction.

In order to achieve an even surface finish to the partition, all the members of the framework should be of equal thickness, the common sizes of members being 100 mm x 50 mm, 100 mm x 38 mm, 75 mm x 50 mm and 75 mm x 38 mm.

Openings are formed by nailing a head-piece across the opening between two studs. A stronger construction may be achieved by increasing the size of the studs forming the jambs of the opening or by constructing a separate framework of jambs which support the head-piece (fig. 13.2). A further alternative is to incorporate a storey-height door set into the framework.

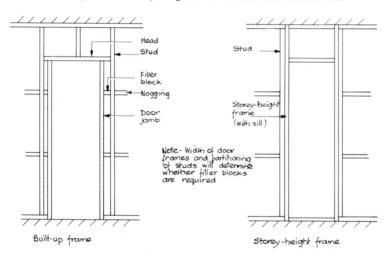

Fig. 13.2 Openings

By virtue of its open framework, the partition will easily accommodate services (fig. 13.3), and notches are cut or holes drilled for cables or pipework. Battens are also fitted in the framework to provide a fixing for items such as light switches, power points, or wash-basins. Thermal and sound insulation can be improved by incorporating mineral quilting in the gaps of the framework after one side of the framework has been lined.

113

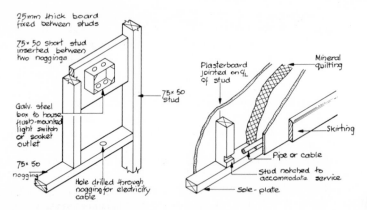

Fig. 13.3 Incorporating services

A 12.5 m plasterboard lining is fixed to the studding with galvanised nails, and the jointing of the sheets (fig. 13.4) will depend on the shaped sheet edge (tapered, bevelled, or square). The boards should be butted together and a layer of joint filler applied; special paper tape is then bedded into the filler and another coat of filler is applied, the edges being smoothed off with a sponge. When the filler has hardened, a further coating of joint finish is applied in a 200 to 250 mm wide-strip and again is smoothed off with a sponge. Finally, the whole surface of the wall should be sponged with a thin slurry of joint finish.

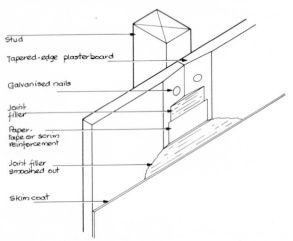

Fig. 13.4 Plasterboard jointing

Finishes to the partition in the form of skirtings and architraves are very easily fixed by nailing them to the studs, head-piece, or sole-plates.

114

14   Stairs and landings

Understands the construction of stairs with landings.

14.1   Sketches typical layouts of stairs with landings.
14.2   Sketches and describes the construction of stairs with landings.

Acknowledgement is due to the Technician Education Council for permission to use the content of the TEC units in this chapter. The council reserves the right to amend the content of its units at any time.

14.1 Landings

The requirements of the Building Regulations (section K) relating to landings are (fig. 14.1):

a) there shall be no more than sixteen rises per flight of steps if the stairway serves an area used for shop or assembly purposes;

b) there shall be no more than thirty-six rises in consecutive flights without a change in direction of travel of 30° or more;

c) the going of a landing shall be not less than the width of a stairway;

d) the top of any balustrade guarding a landing at the top of a flight shall be a minimum height of 900 mm for a private stairway or 1000 mm for a common stairway and 1100 mm for other stairways.

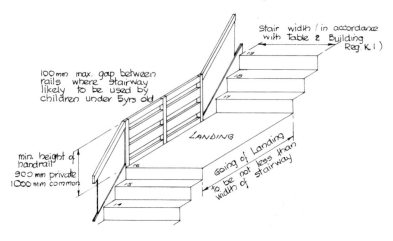

Fig. 14.1   Regulations

Landings may also be incorporated in stair construction when there is insufficient room in the plan layout for the construction of a straight flight.

The terms 'quarter' and 'half' in landing or stair terminology refer to that part of a circle through which the direction of travel is changed; for example, a quarter-space landing is one where the direction of travel changes through $\frac{1}{4}$ circle or 90° (fig. 14.2).

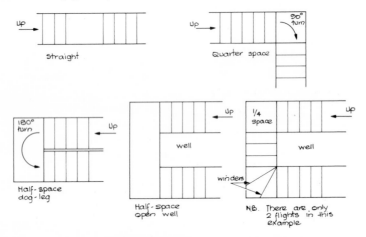

Fig. 14.2 Landing terminology

It should be noted that changes of direction may also be accomplished by means of winders, but there are then further regulations to be observed (section H3 (4)(g) and section J of the table relating to regulation H3).

14.2 Landing construction

The landing must support the weight of the people and goods using it, together with any loads which may be transferred from the straight flight(s) to it.

The landing is effectively a suspended floor and is constructed in a similar manner (fig. 14.3). The joists will generally be of smaller section, since their span is less than the normal floor joist, and are known as landing or bridging joists.

In a quarter-space landing, the corner of the landing adjacent to the newel does not have any direct support unless a wall or framework is constructed under the outer string of the lower flight. The newel drop is, therefore, frequently taken down to the ground floor to provide the required support and is known as the storey newel. An alternative to the direct support is the provision of a cantilever support, built into the wall at one end and supported at mid-length by a diagonal bearer built into the adjoining walls (fig. 14.4).

In the design of any landing, the adjacent walls must not only be able to support the vertical loads but must also resist the lateral thrust exerted by the strings and carriages (fig. 14.5).

116

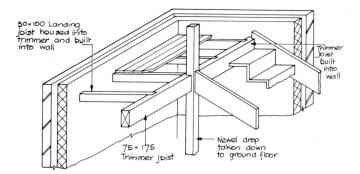

Fig. 14.3 Landing construction

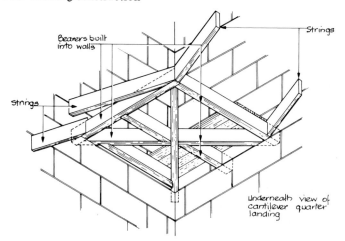

Fig. 14.4 Landing construction

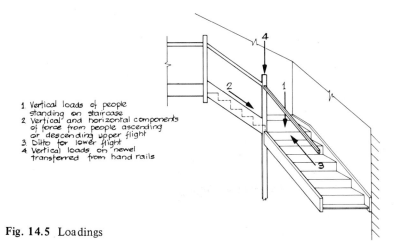

Fig. 14.5 Loadings

117

15 Doors

Understands the main factors affecting the choice of doors and draws typical details.

15.1 Identifies main factors affecting choice of door type.
15.2 Prepares door schedule including ironmongery from drawing and trade literature.
15.3 Sketches and describes typical internal door details at head and jamb including fixing, provision for second fixings and furnishings.
15.4 Sketches and describes typical external door details at head, jamb and threshold including fixings and finishings.

Acknowledgement is due to the Technician Education Council for permission to use the content of the TEC units in this chapter. The council reserves the right to amend the content of its units at any time.

15.1 Selection of doors
The main factors affecting the choice of doors are:
a) *Position in the building*   The requirements of an external door vary considerably from those of an internal door.
b) The order of priority of the performance requirements of a door.
   i) *Weather exclusion*
   ii) *Security*
   iii) *Fire*
   iv) *Thermal and sound insulation*
   v) *Privacy*
   vi) *Durability*
   vii) *Method of operation*
c) *Appearance*   The appearance of a domestic bathroom door is of little consequence, whereas the doors to the office of a managing director of a large company should create a suitable impression on those entering.

15.2 Door schedules
The preparation of a door schedule, as with the window schedule detailed in section 11.2, complements the information detailed on the drawings and in a bill of quantities. A typical schedule is shown in fig. 15.1.

15.3 Internal doors
Internal doors are incorporated after the work of constructing the walls, roof, and floors has been completed.

DOOR SCHEDULE
FOR
HOUSE TYPE B.3.

Door	Basic size		Lintel	Frame	Door Type/Finish	Ironmongery	Notes
	Height	Width					
D1	2100	1500	CNP 3	VS9 C29	DR 19 CDS 29	Messrs B & P FD pack No.1 + Messrs C.D barrel bolt No A50Y	OQ glazing to screen
D2	2100	900	CNP 3	FNS 29	DR 10 D 29	Messrs B & P BD pack No.1 + Messrs CD barrel bolt No. A 5 3 Z	Obscured glazing to panels
D3	2400	800	–	SH Left H	Teak	Messrs B & P ID pack No.1	OQ glazed fanlight
D4	2400	800	~	as D3	Teak	as D3	as D3
D5	2400	800	~	as D3	Teak	as D3	as D3
D6	2400	700	–	SH Right H	Teak	Messrs B & P BR pack No.1	as D3
D7	2100	600	–	4DF20	FDP 20	as D3	–
D8	2100	800	–	DH Left H	Sapele	as D3	–
D9	2100	800	–	as D8	Sapele	as D3	–
D10	2100	800	~	as D8	Sapele	as D3	–
D11	2100	800	–	DH Right H	Plus coat	as D6	–
D12	2100	700	–	as D11	Plus coat	as D6	–
D13	2100	600	~	as D8	Plus coat	as D3	–

Fig. 15.1 Typical door schedule

It has already been stated (Volume 1, section 9.3) that the modern method of construction is to use factory-made door sets which are delivered to site with the frame fully assembled and the door complete with its ironmongery, already hung. In such a case, the work of installation is carried out by a joiner at the *second-fix* stage, as follows.

a) The door is removed from the frame and is carefully stored. Lift-off rising-butt or special snap-in hinges are used to facilitate this operation, rather than unscrewing the hinge from the door or frame.

b) The frame is located in position and is wedged using folding wedges, ensuring that the frame is both plumb and square.

It should be noted that frames may be supplied with or without a flat threshold; those without a threshold have a mild-steel dowel driven into the bottom of the jamb. This dowel projects below the base of the jamb and is grouted into preformed holes in the floor or is cast into the subsequent floor screeding.

c) Holes are drilled through the frame into the wall jamb, and any necessary packing is inserted between the frame and wall.

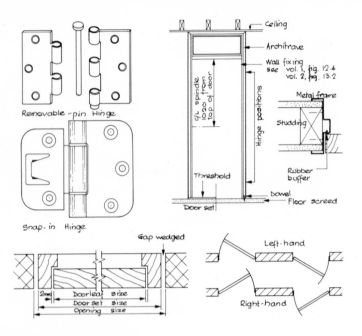

Fig. 15.2 Internal door details

d) The frame is then securely fixed using wood screws. (In the case of a brick or block wall, timber fixing slips should have been previously built into the wall — see Volume 1, fig. 12.4 — but where this has not been done, timber or plastics plugs are inserted into the holes drilled into the wall and the screws are driven into them.)
e) The door is rehung to ensure that it operates freely, and the frame is adjusted to provide a 2 mm door clearance all round.

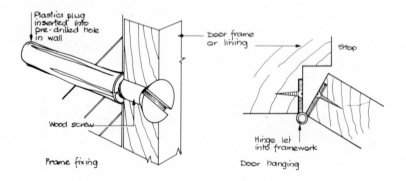

Fig. 15.3 Fixings

120

f) The architraves, which are generally provided with the door set, are fixed to the jamb using oval nails which are punched home. The cross-section of the architraves depends on the wall thickness and on the thickness of the frame of the door set (see Volume 1, fig. 9.14).

g) The door is again removed and is stored until the *final-fix* operation, to avoid damage.

Where door frames are used in walls which are finished with traditional plastering, the architrave is fixed after the plasterwork has set hard.

Where door sets are not used, a lining is constructed in the opening and is anchored to the wall as in (d) above. The stop is then fixed to the lining if the lining itself has not already been rebated to form the stop. The door is then offered into the frame to check for clearance. Hinges are first fixed to the door, the stile being rebated to accommodate the thickness of the hinge. The door is again offered to the frame, the hinge is fixed to the frame, and finally the door is checked for smooth operation and is eased as required.

Other ironmongery required, e.g. mortice latch, lever handle, striking plate, is finally added to complete the door. BS 5872:1980 gives the recommended sizes of locks and latches for doors, while the requirements relating to hinges can be found in BS 1227:part 1A:1967.

15.4 External doors
External doors are fixed into the opening in a similar manner to that described in section 15.3.

The treatment of the opening has already been described in sections 8.5 to 8.7, while the treatment at the head and jamb is very similar to that outlined for windows in section 11.3.

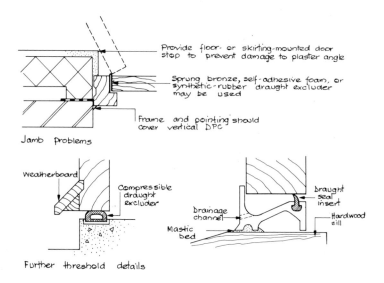

Fig. 15.4 External door details

The major problem in the treatment of an external door is at the threshold. Since it is common practice for the door to open inwards, the rain, especially driving rain, must be prevented from entering the premises at the bottom of the door. There are two conventional methods of dealing with the problem.

a) A 3 mm-thick galvanised-metal water bar is let into the top of the threshold and is sealed in. The bottom rail of the door is rebated over the weather bar. Doors in exposed situations are also fitted with further protection in the form of a weather-board which may be housed or tongued into the external face of the bottom rail.

b) A preformed metal strip (known as a 'Macclesfield' sill) is screwed to a flat or weathered hardwood sill. This forms the stop at the bottom of the door, but also allows rain-water running down the door to drain out through weep holes, while at the same time a synthetic rubber insert provides a draught seal at the bottom of the door.

External doors are required to provide security, which implies some form of locking device (fig. 15.5). The most secure forms of locks are those which are morticed into the frame rather than being surface mounted (rim), and have a large number of levers — the greater the number of levers to be moved by a key, the more accurate must be the key. The mortice for the lock having been formed, holes are drilled in the stile to form the keyhole. The popular alternative to a mortice lock is the cylinder night latch. The cylinder is housed in a 40 mm diameter hole drilled through the door, and the latch surface is mounted on the inside.

Other holes may be drilled through the stile, middle rail, muntin, etc. to allow for delivery of letters and newspapers, the provision of an optical spy hole, and a door bell.

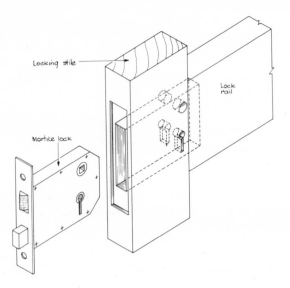

Fig. 15.5 Locks

16   Ceilings

Understands the construction of ceilings to timber and concrete soffits.

16.1   Explains methods of forming ceilings with plasterboard.

Acknowledgement is due to the Technician Education Council for permission to use the content of the TEC units in this chapter. The council reserves the right to amend the content of its units at any time.

16.1 Plasterboard ceilings

There are two main thicknesses of plasterboard: 12.7 mm, which is used for wall linings, and 9.5 mm which, since it is lighter in weight and not able to resist as much physical damage, is used for the lining of ceilings.

The boards are fixed to the joist soffits by galvanised plasterboard nails at 150 mm centres, with the cross-joints staggered (fig. 16.1). The joints

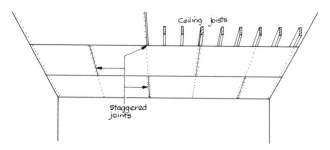

Fig. 16.1 Board layout

between the boards, especially the square-edged boards, are reinforced with jute scrim approximately 90 mm wide, to prevent cracks occurring in the covering skim coat which is only some 5 mm in thickness (fig. 16.2). Cracking is, however, most likely to occur at the junction between the walls and the ceiling. This junction can also be reinforced by fixing scrim in the angle, but a better method is to run a traditional cornice using plaster or cast fibrous plaster. An even better alternative is to mask the joint with a specially preformed plasterboard coving (fig. 16.3), and this is fixed to the ceiling and wall using galvanised nails or screws at approximately 600 mm centres in the joists and at 300 mm centres to plugs fixed in the wall. An alternative fixing is by the use of special adhesives, provided that the background is suitable.

123

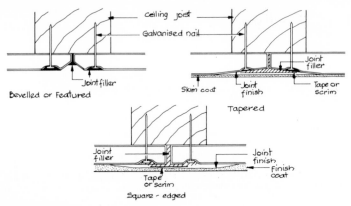

Fig. 16.2 Jointing

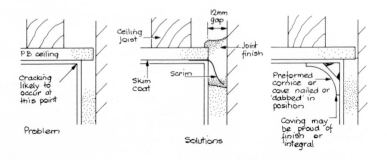

Fig. 16.3 Cornice details

Ceilings below solid, in-situ, or precast concrete floors are generally finished with either one-, two-, or three-coat plasterwork or special crack-resistant plastics ceiling coatings; but a plasterboard lining may be fixed to timber battens in a similar manner to that used for a suspended timber floor. These timber battens may be fixed either directly to the concrete soffit, using nails fired from a cartridge tool, or to clips or timber pads cast in the concrete during pouring (fig. 16.4).

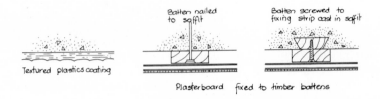

Fig. 16.4 Ceilings to concrete soffits

124

17   Plasterwork

Describes plaster finishings and their application.

17.1   Describes the characteristics of plaster finishings.
17.2   Explains which backgrounds are suitable for BS types of plaster.
17.3   Describes the mixing and application of plaster.

Acknowledgement is due to the Technician Education Council for permission to use the content of the TEC units in this chapter. The council reserves the right to amend the content of its units at any time.

Plaster derived from gypsum was used by the Egyptians over 4000 years ago. They found it to be tough, hard-setting, and long-lasting. The use of plaster for fire protection was recognised in Britain immediately after the fire which destroyed London Bridge in 1212, when King John issued an edict to the effect that all shops on the Thames be plastered and whitewashed 'within and without'.

The traditional plaster in this country was *lime plaster*. This, although readily available from natural limestone, contains many impurities such as silica, sulphur, and alumina. These impurities greatly affect such properties of the lime plaster as setting time, workability, strength, and shrinkage, the latter being a major problem with this type of plaster.

The *gypsum plasters* are obtained by mining the natural gypsum rock, crushing it to a powder, and heating it to approximately $150^{\circ}C$ to drive out the majority of the water present in the material. The material at this stage is known as a *hemi-hydrate plaster* or *plaster of Paris*. Water reintroduced to the material causes the gypsum rock to be reformed. Setting time for plaster of Paris is too quick to be suitable for normal plastering work, but, by the addition of chemical retarding agents, a delayed set can be achieved — such plasters are known as *retarded hemi-hydrate plasters*.

By varying the temperature at which the water is driven off from the natural crushed rock, the particle size of the powder, or the additives used, a variety of plasters can be produced for specific uses.

17.1 Characteristics of plaster finishes
The functions of a plaster finish are
a) to cover up uneven backgrounds,
b) to provide a smooth surface,
c) to provide a hygienic surface,
d) to accept a decorative finish,

e) to provide resistance to fire,
f) to provide sound insulation,
g) to provide thermal insulation,
h) to resist surface abrasion or damage,
j) to adhere permanently to the background.

No single plaster can fulfil all the above functions, hence a number of varieties are manufactured and classified in BS 5492:1977, together with their characteristics.

Gypsum plasters

Class A   *Plaster of Paris* (BS 1191:part 1:1973)   Sets too quickly; unsuitable for most jobs other than small repair work. May be gauged with lime. Avoid overtrowelling. Used in the mouldings of friezes with hessian as reinforcement.

Class B   *Retarded hemi-hydrate plaster* (BS 1191:part 1:1973)   Generally used as a binder with a fine aggregate such as sand. Should be allowed to dry as quickly as possible. A small amount of expansion takes place on setting. Should not be retempered after initial setting. Addition of lime will accelerate the set but will increase the workability (a maximum of 25% of the mix volume may be lime).

Used in the manufacture of plasterboards, and also neat as a finish to plasterboarding.

Class C   *Anhydrous gypsum plaster* (BS 1191:part 1:1973)   Has all water driven off from the rock during manufacture. Slow setting, but provides a harder surface finish than Class B.

Suitable for finish to sanded gypsum or 1:1:6 cement:lime: sand undercoats, but not suitable for finishing to plasterboard or insulating fibreboard.

Class D   *Keene's plaster* (BS 1191:part 1:1973)   This plaster is calcined at higher temperatures and has accelerators added. Lime should never be added.

Used as a final single-coat material. Can be worked to a perfectly true surface.

Final set harder than other plasters. Should not be allowed to dry out too quickly. Suitable for areas where the surface is liable to damage, such as corridors, external angles, etc., and also for areas subject to surface lighting or decoration with gloss paint.

Premixed lightweight plaster (BS 1191:part 2:1973)   There are a number of mixes which use different aggregates (expanded perlite or exfoliated vermiculite) combined with a Class-B plaster to give lighter weight for a given volume, ease of working for the plasterer, higher mixing-water content and hence slower drying, similar surface hardness to Class-B plaster, improved fire resistance, and prevention of condensation.

Type (a): *Undercoat plasters*
  i) Browning — perlite aggregate; suitable for most backgrounds.

Plasters	Shrinkage or expansion	Strength and hardness	Remarks
Lime:sand 1:2 to 3	All shrink on drying	Weak and soft	Takes a long time to harden.
Cement-based undercoats Cement:sand 1:3 to 4	Contents of clay or fine material should not exceed 5%	Strong and hard	Hardens fairly quickly. Undercoats should be allowed to dry thoroughly before applying the next coat.
Cement:lime:sand 1:1:6 1:2:9 Masonry cement:sand 1:4½		Sufficiently strong and hard for most purposes, although the 1:2:9 cement:lime:sand mixes are not sufficiently strong to receive neat gypsum-plaster finishes.	Hardens slowly. Undercoats should be allowed to dry as above.
Premixed lightweight cement undercoat	Shrinks on drying.	Sufficiently strong and hard for most purposes	Hardens slowly. Undercoats should be allowed to dry as above.
Gypsum-plaster undercoats Class-B plaster:sand 1:1 to 3	The addition of sand reduces expansion.	Strength falls off steeply with increase in sand content.	Sets quickly.
Premixed lightweight gypsum undercoats	Their relatively small movement is easily restrained by the backings.	Varies with the type of undercoat.	Sets quickly. It is essential to use the undercoat appropriate to the background.

Fig. 17.1 Characteristics of plaster undercoats

ii) Metal lathing — mixture of perlite and vermiculite aggregates; special backgrounds only.

iii) Bonding — vermiculite aggregate; backgrounds where adhesion is a problem, such as engineering brickwork or aerated concrete.

Type (b): *Final-coat plaster*

Finish plaster — in all cases similar to Class B; excessive use of water and trowel will cause surface crazing.

Special plasters

Single-coat, thin coat, or thin wall   Not as strong as Class B, but similar characteristics. Not suitable for backgrounds such as woodwool slabs, fibre insulation board, strawboard, and some concretes such as 'no-fines'. Must have suitable background or undercoat. Can be sprayed.

Acoustic   Incorporates aggregate such as pumice. Undercoat must be suitable and provide a good key. Various textured finishes can be incorporated — care required in method of decorating if texturing is not to be 'filled in'.

Projection   Specially formulated for machine spraying. Good key required. Sufficiently hard and strong for most purposes. Quicker finishing than two-coat systems. Correct grading of aggregates required when premixed material not used.

X-ray   Provides protection in X-ray installations — incorporates barytes (barium sulphate) aggregates in both undercoat and finish materials.

Cement plasters

These contain cement, lime, and sand, the proportions (by volume) varying according to requirements. All varieties shrink on drying, and adequate drying time should be allowed between coats. To avoid major problems, the coats should be of similar composition, the sand well graded, and overworking avoided. The 1:3 or 1:$\frac{1}{4}$:3 mix provides a very strong hard material; the 1:1:6 mix is slightly weaker but retains the hardness; while the 1:2:9 mix is very weak all round.

17.2 Backgrounds

There are a number of background characteristics to be considered when selecting a suitable plastering system.

a) *Strength*   The strength of the undercoat should be less than that of the background.

b) *Porosity and suction*   Both affect the adhesion of the plaster system to the background and therefore its ultimate strength.

c) *Bond*   The plaster must be able to key to the surface. This key may be provided either artificially by raking out the mortar joints in blockwork or naturally by the background material itself, as in the case of no-fines concrete.

d) *Trueness of construction*   Since plaster is required to provide a smooth surface, excessive filling of surface undulations may require a number of coats, as too thick a layer of plaster will affect its adhesion characteristics.

Background	Undercoat (see key below)	Finishing (see key below)
Brickwork and building blocks generally	1 or 4	A
	2, 3, 5, 6, or 7	A, B, C, D, or F
In-situ concrete	5, 6, or 7	A, B, C, D, or F
	None	C
Wood laths	1 or 4	A
	5, 6, or 7	A, B, C, D, or F
Metal lathing	1 or 4	A
	5 or 7	A, B, C, D, or F
Gypsum plasterboard and fibre building board	5	A, B, C, D, or F
	None	C
Wood-wool slabs	1 or 4	A
	2, 5, 6, or 7	A, B, C, D, or F

Key

Undercoats

1. Cement/lime/sand 1:2:9 by volume
2. Cement/lime/sand 1:1:6 by volume
3. Cement/sand
4. Gypsum plaster gauged lime/sand
5. Retarded hemi-hydrate gypsum plaster/sand
6. Anhydrous gypsum plaster/sand
7. Lime-gauged anhydrous gypsum plaster/sand

Finishing coats

A. Lime putty gauged with gypsum plaster ($\frac{1}{4}$ to $\frac{1}{2}$ vol. gypsum plaster to 1 vol. lime putty)
B. Lime putty gauged with gypsum plaster ($\frac{1}{4}$ to 1 vol. gypsum plaster to 1 vol. lime putty)
C. Retarded hemi-hydrate gypsum plaster
D. Anhydrous gypsum plaster, Keene's or Parian
F. Retarded hemi-hydrate gypsum plaster or anhydrous gypsum plaster gauged with lime

Fig. 17.2 Suitable undercoats and finishing coats for various backgrounds. For more detailed information, refer to BS 5492:1977, table 2

e) *Soluble salts*   Where large amounts of water have been used in the background construction (e.g. brickwork, blockwork, in-situ concrete), the drying out may result in these salts being brought to the surface in the form of efflorescence after plastering.

f) *Thermal and moisture movement*   Differing amounts of movement may occur between the background and undercoat, resulting in a loss of adhesion or cracking of the plaster.

Types of background

BS 5492:1977 classifies the types of background as follows.

a) *Solid*
   i) Dense, strong, smooth materials — these include high-density clay or concrete bricks and blocks and dense precast or in-situ concrete.
   ii) Moderately strong and porous materials such as most clay and concrete bricks and blocks, calcium-silicate bricks, and medium-density concrete.
   iii) Moderately weak and porous materials, which include weak bricks and lightweight concrete blocks.
   iv) No-fines concrete.

b) *Slabs*   These are dry linings such as woodwool, cork, and compressed-straw slabs.

c) *Boards*   Plasterboard and expanded plastics boards comprise this section.

d) *Metal lathing and decking*

e) *Painted and tiled surfaces*

Suitable BS plasters

The selection of a suitable plaster for a particular background depends on the type and characteristics of the given background (see fig. 17.2).

In general, very dense smooth surfaces such as concrete or tiles will require the application of a bonding agent before plastering. Suitable bonding agents are emulsions of PVAC or other polymers, or bituminous emulsions. The bituminous varieties are not recommended for soffit work, but provide a d.p.m. as an additional benefit when applied to walls.

Different backgrounds may be encountered on a given surface area, and in such cases additional reinforcement in the form of galvanised expanded-metal lathing or scrim should be used to prevent differential-movement cracks occuring (fig. 17.3). (Small areas may be completely isolated from the background and bridged over using reinforcement.)

17.3 Mixing and application of plaster

a) Mixing

The mixing of the materials may be carried out by hand in large open tubs or, more commonly, in small mechanical mixers similar to those used for mixing mortar. The proportions of the ingredients (when not premixed) are measured by volume using gauge boxes (see fig. 6.5). Overmixing should be avoided, since this may accelerate the setting, especially where gypsum plasters are concerned.

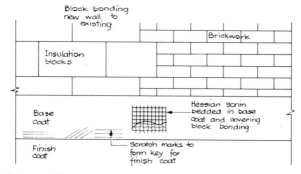

Fig. 17.3 Scrim reinforcement

Expanded metal lathing attached to soffit of combined steel lintel to receive plaster finish

b) Application

Plaster is applied to a surface in one, two, or three coats by hand using a float, darby, and trowel (fig. 17.4). The plasterer applies the plaster to the wall by means of a float from the hawk or handboard; an area is then straight-

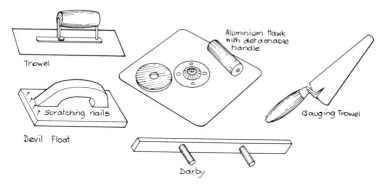

Fig. 17.4 Tools

ened off using the darby and is smoothed over using the wooden or steel trowel. If the coat being applied is an undercoat, the surface will be scratched before it hardens, using a comb or other implement, in order to provide a key for the subsequent coat.

One-coat work   This is generally used for skimming or setting coats on board or slab backgrounds or on straight backgrounds such as precast concrete. The advantages of this method are (i) a reduction in the cost of labour and materials, (ii) a reduction in the weight of the surface finish, and (iii) a reduction in bonding problems as a result of the reduced weight. It is, however, better to use two-coat work on uneven surfaces. Single-coat work dries out more rapidly, thus allowing earlier decoration.

Two-coat work   The undercoat or floating coat is usually some 8 to 10 mm thick and, when scratched and allowed to set, is covered by a 2 to 3 mm finishing or skimming coat. BS 5492 states that the total thickness on 'backgrounds other than concrete exclusive of keys or dubbing out should be of the order of 13 mm. On concrete this thickness should not exceed 10 mm unless a mechanical key is provided.'

When using the premixed 'Thistle' or 'Carlite' plasters, a finish coat can be applied only 90 minutes after the application of the floating coat.

Three-coat work   This method is used where large surface irregularities are present or where the plaster is being applied to lathing. It is also preferable where a high-class finish is required on brickwork, since the initial or rendering coat not only takes up surface irregularities but also reduces suction variations caused by the background.

The overall thickness of this work should not exceed 19 mm, and on lathing the thickness should not exceed about 12 mm.

Spray plaster   The plaster is mixed and pumped to the nozzle in a mobile machine, and water is added automatically to give an even and correct consistency. Projection plaster is specifically designed for spray application and will adhere to most backgrounds. It replaces the normal two-and three-coat work with a single application. The plaster is thixotropic and remains workable after spraying for sufficient time to allow straightening and smoothing off.

Treatment at angles   External angles are more likely to suffer damage from knocks and abrasion than internal angles and are therefore provided with additional protection in the form of galvanised metal angle beads (fig. 17.5), which also assist in forming straight arrises. The beads are fixed by first applying plaster dabs on each side of the angle at approximately 600 mm intervals; the expanded metal wings of the bead are then pressed into the dabs and the angle is plumbed using a straight edge. The floating coat is then applied to the wall surface up to the bead so that it is just below the level

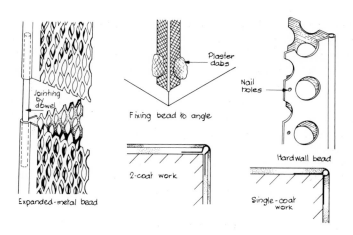

Jointing
by
dowel

Plaster
dabs

Fixing bead to angle

Nail
holes

Expanded-metal bead

2-coat work

Hardwall bead

Single-coat
work

Fig. 17.5 Angle beads

of the bead nosing and, when this coat is set, the finish coat is applied so that
it just covers the bead nosing.

Internal angles are normally finished square and are formed by hand, the
plasterer using a steel finishing trowel to obtain the 'sharp' angle.

18   Wall tiling

Identifies and understands the application of wall tiling.

18.1   Identifies types and sizes of tiles in common use.
18.2   Explains which backgrounds are suitable to receive tiles.
18.3   Describes the methods of fixing and grouting tiles.

Acknowledgement is due to the Technician Education Council for permission to use the content of the TEC units in this chapter. The council reserves the right to amend the content of its units at any time.

18.1 Tiles

Wall tiles may be classified by the material from which they are made, the finish, and the shape and size. They are used to improve the appearance of a wall, to provide additional resistance to moisture staining or abrasion, or to improve sound and thermal insulation.

a) Materials

i) *Ceramic*   A hard tile which may be cracked by a hard impact, but which provides good resistance to moisture, chemicals, and stains.

ii) *Stainless steel*   Generally used for decorative purposes, but also found in areas where hygiene is important, such as in kitchens.

iii) *Plastics*   There are many varieties of plastics, the most well known of which, in tile form, is expanded polystyrene.

iv) *Glass*   Usually in the form of mirror tiles, which may be used to give a large-mirror effect or to highlight displays, but also used in a smaller form.

v) *Mosaic*   Molten glass with pigments pressed in moulds to produce units of small size, 20 mm x 20 mm x 3 mm. Generally available reverse-mounted on paper in square flat sheets.

Other tile materials are those which are normally used on floors but which can be continued up the walls. These include

vi) *Cork*

vii) *Linoleum*

viii) *Marble*

ix) *Quarry*

x) *Rubber*

xi) *Fibreboard*

b) Finishes

i) *Glazed* On ceramic tiles there are two types of glaze: earthenware and coloured enamels. The earthenware glazes are white or cream, but there are a wide variety of plain and mottled colours available in the enamelled finish, which can have a glossy, eggshell, or matt surface.

ii) *Glossy* ⎫ These finishes can be obtained on most of the wall-tile
iii) *Matt* ⎭ materials.

iv) *Textured* Ceramic tiles may be obtained with a ripple form on the surface.

v) *Profiled* The tiles have a moulded face which is available in a variety of standard designs.

c) Shape

The standard tiles are rectangular, but hexagonal ones are available and they can all have various edge finishes (fig. 18.1). Special tiles provide a suitable finish at angles and exposed edges, and, in addition, special fittings are available for holding soap, toilet rolls, and other accessories.

i) *Square edge* Generally available only on the thicker tiles.

ii) *Cushion edge* The tiles have a slight rounding at the glazed edges — this helps to even out surface variations.

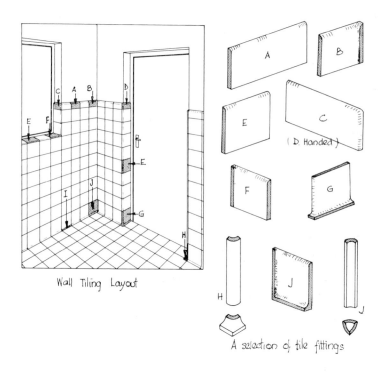

Wall Tiling Layout

A selection of tile fittings

Fig. 18.1 Tile details

135

iii) *Round edge*   The tiles have a definite rounding on one or two edges. They provide the cheapest method of terminating a tiled area.

iv) *Spacer lugs*   Incorporated on the tile edge, they maintain a standard 3 mm joint width between tiles and also provide a crushing point which will fail in compression without damaging the tile.

v) *Attached angle tiles*   Having a rounded short return on one or two sides, they are used at external or internal angles.

vi) *Beads and coves*   Narrow curved tiles used at external or internal angles respectively, as an alternative to (v) above.

vii) *Capping*   A narrow tile with one or two rounded edges, used in place of (iii) above.

d) Standards

BS 6431 consists of a number of parts which relate to ceramic floor and wall tiles. It details methods of testing for a wide range of aspects which include absorption; dimensional accuracy; surface quality; thermal expansion; and abrasion, chemical, and frost resistance.

Sizes are generally based on the 100 mm standard module or multiples thereof, with allowances being made by the manufacturer for joint widths.

18.2 Backgrounds

Tiles can be fixed to a wide range of backgrounds but, since the fixing is by adhesion, the background must be strong enough to support the tile weight without losing adhesion itself. The background should also be stable in respect of expansion or shrinkage resulting from structural, thermal, or moisture movement, since any movement will cause tiling failure — this is most important where tiling is carried out on differing backgrounds. The background should therefore be dry, rigid, and — ideally — smooth. Suitable backgrounds are as follows.

a) *Sand–cement rendering*   A 1:3 or 1:4 mix of ordinary Portland cement and sand is ideal — a richer mix will tend to shrink and crack, while a leaner mix will have insufficient strength to support the weight of tiles. The rendering should not be thicker than approximately 12 mm, but, if the background surface has large undulations requiring a greater thickness, the render should be built up in two or more coats, each coat being not more than 10 mm thick and allowed to dry out before a further coat is applied. It is recommended that a final coat of render should be allowed to dry out for at least 7 days but preferably 14 days.

b) *Plasterwork*   It is essential that there is good adhesion between the plasterwork and the wall behind, especially if lightweight plaster or lightweight wall blocks are involved. As a large amount of water is involved in plasterwork, at least 4 weeks should be allowed for drying out before tiling is begun. Old or dusty surfaces will need a binding coat of a suitable primer brushed over them. It should be noted that plaster cannot be regarded as a satisfactory background for tiling in wet areas such as shower compartments.

c) *Sheets and boards* (plasterboard, hardboard, plywood, chipboard, blockboard, asbestos board, etc.) Boarding provides a suitable background for tiles, especially where there is a rough but clean side available. The most important consideration, however, is that of springiness and surface deflection, as a rigid flat surface is required. This can be obtained by adequate bracing – 75 mm x 50 mm studs at 300 mm centres both horizontally and vertically, with the boards screwed rather than nailed to the studs.

d) *Painted surfaces* Gloss paint, provided there is good adhesion between the paint and the surface to which it is applied, provides an adequate background. Flaking gloss paint, distemper, emulsion, or lime-wash have poor adhesion and should be removed mechanically rather than by a paint stripper.

e) *Glazed tiles or bricks* Provided that they are clean, have good adhesion to their own background, and present a smooth surface, these materials provide an adequate background.

In all cases, a floating coat of cement–sand rendering should be applied as described previously in section (a). BS 5385:part 1:1976 and part 2: 1978 recommended suitable mixes for the various backgrounds.

18.3 Fixing and grouting

a) Fixing
The selection of a suitable adhesive depends on the nature of the background and the duty and location of the tiling. BS 5385:part 1:1976 and part 2: 1978 recommend performance standards for various types of adhesive.

i) *Thin-bed method* (fig. 18.2) Suitable for dry interior situations where where there is a true plane surface. The method is to apply a 3 mm coating of cement-based mortar or mastic adhesive to the background and

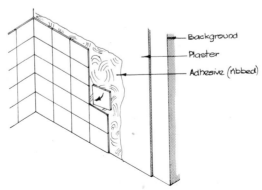

Background
Plaster
Adhesive (ribbed)

Fig. 18.2 Tile fixing (thin bed)

137

then, after spreading over an area not exceeding lm^2, ribbing the adhesive with a notched trowel. The tiles, fixed dry, are then pressed into the adhesive and positioned using a twisting/sliding action — this ensures good adhesion. Where the tiles have spacer lugs, the correct joint size will automatically be given; for tiles without lugs, a 1.5 mm joint must be left around each tile. Surplus adhesive on the tile face and between the joints should be removed before the joints are grouted.

This method is suitable on plaster, paint, glazed tiles and bricks, metal, and rendered surfaces on a backing of common brickwork or blockwork or lightweight concrete blocks.

ii) *Solid-bed method* (fig. 18.3)   Used for areas where water penetration is possible, such as showers and swimming pools, it is essential to prevent moisture penetration behind the tile. The adhesive is not ribbed, and the dry tiles are pressed straight on to the 3 mm adhesive bed and are tapped firmly into position, thus avoiding air pockets behind the tiles.

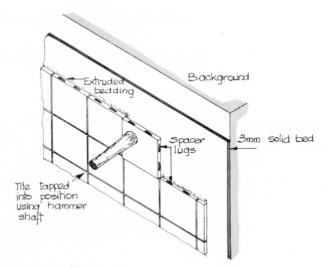

Fig. 18.3 Tile fixing (solid bed)

iii) *Thick-bed method* (fig. 18.4)   Used where the background surface is not flat enough to use the thin-bed method. Dry tiles are fixed using a mastic adhesive in a similar manner to (ii) above. Alternatively, a 1:4 cement—sand mix is applied to the wall or is buttered on to the back of the tiles. The tiles in this case should be soaked for at least 30 minutes in clean water and allowed to drain — this ensures that there is no loss of moisture from the mix into the tile, which would reduce the strength and adhesion of the mix. The tiles are then fixed as before.

In both cases there should be a minimum 6.5 mm thickness of adhesive (this is especially important where mechanical damage may occur), and the tiles should be cleaned off after approximately two hours.

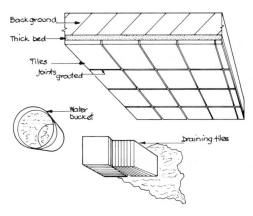

Fig. 18.4 Tile fixing (thick bed)

Where necessary, cutting of tiles is done by a special guillotine or by scoring the face and breaking the tile across. Additional care should be taken when fitting tiles into corners and around holes or other obstructions.

b) Grouting
The joints between tiles must be able to accommodate small movements and the material used must not be too strong; hence neat cement should not be used — there are many proprietary brands of grouting available. Grouting should never be begun until the adhesive has set — this can take up to 24 hours for normal tiling, but where the background has a low porosity, such as paint, up to 3 days should be allowed.

The grout is pressed firmly into the joints and around the edges of the tiles and is packed in with a pointed stick having a thickness equivalent to the size of the joint. By applying a second coat some 24 hours after the initial jointing, the permeability of the joint will be reduced (suitable for showers etc.). The excess grout should be scraped off the tiles and the surface be wiped down with a damp sponge and then polished with a clean dry cloth.

c) Movement joints
Any movement of the tiling may cause damage to the surface. In order to avoid this problem, movement joints should be included (fig. 18.5). These joints should be located where there are structural movement joints, at 3 to 5 m both horizontally and vertically, at internal vertical angles, and where tiling abuts different backgrounds.

The joint should be at least 6 mm wide, continuous throughout the tiling and bed, kept free from dirt and adhesive, and filled with an elastomeric mastic such as butyl rubber, silicone-rubber sealant, or a polysulphide compound.

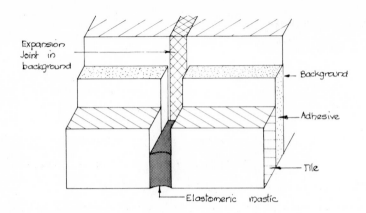

Fig. 18.5 Movement joints

19   Paints

Understands the properties of paints and techniques of application.

19.1 Identifies and describes the properties of oil and water-bound paints used for protection and decoration.

19.2 Describes the application of paint by brush, roller and spray.

Acknowledgement is due to the Technician Education Council for permission to use the content of the TEC units in this chapter. The council reserves the right to amend the content of its units at any time.

Paint is a liquid which, when spread on a surface in a thin film, dries into a hard tough but elastic skin. This skin provides protection and decoration to many building materials, thereby enhancing their appearance and increasing their durability.

The functions of a paint or paint system are

a) to protect surfaces from rain, sunlight, abrasion, chemicals, micro-organisms, insects, fungi, and fire;

b) to provide decoration in the form of colour, light diffusion, and area definition;

c) to provide hygienic surfaces;

d) to provide antistatic properties;

e) to absorb sound.

In fulfilling one or more of the above functions, the paint must also be able to

f) remain in contact with the surface to which it has been applied;

g) resist the strains and movement caused by temperature variation and changes in moisture content of the background;

h) be easily applied to the surface, and easily removed when deterioration causes film breakdown.

There are many types of paint available which fulfil many specific as well as general functions. The surface finish represents approximately 5% of the initial cost of a building, but during that building's life the recurring costs of maintenance on the surfaces may well represent 25% of that initial cost. It therefore follows that the use of quality materials and good workmanship in their application can, by increasing the maintenance period, be economic in the long term.

19.1 Properties
Paint has three broadly classified constituents: (a) the vehicle, (b) pigments, and (c) additives.

a) The vehicle

This is the name given to the liquid portion of the paint. It has two components: the binder, or film-former, and the solvent, thinner, or diluent.

The combination of a binder and thinner gives a transparent coating known as a lacquer or varnish.

i) *Binder*   The binder in water-bound paint binds the other ingredients of the paint together, while in an oil-bound paint the ingredients are dispersed into the binder. The binder must also hold the pigment in suspension and adhering to the background and, once applied, convert from a liquid coating to a hard dry elastic skin which provides resistance to water, chemicals, and abrasion (fig. 19.1).

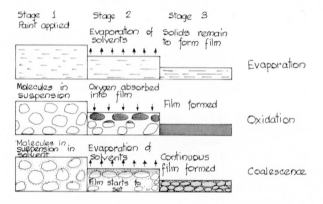

Fig. 19.1 Drying of paint

Common binders include drying oils such as linseed oil, safflower oil, and tung oil; resins such as alkyd, silicone, polyurethane, or epoxy resins; and oleo-resins – natural resins mixed with a drying oil.

ii) *Solvent*   Solvents are added to a paint during manufacture, while thinners are added later.

A solvent dissolves the resinous constituents. A thinner, being a blend of different solvents, dilutes the already dissolved resin and imparts other qualities such as longer wet-edge time. Solvents also alter the viscosity of the paint to suit the particular method of application and surface to be treated, but must evaporate once the coating has been applied. It is from this section of the vehicle that the paint obtains the classification of oil-bound or water-bound.

b) Pigments

Pigments are crystalline particles of organic or inorganic materials. They give the paint body, opacity or hiding power, and colour, and also assist in protecting the surface. The most common white pigment is titanium dioxide, which obliterates the background but is not poisonous. The other white pigment is white lead, which combines well with oil, has good durability and elasticity, and is ideal for the priming of external joinery, where it is mixed by equal volume with red lead to form 'pink' wood primer. White lead is, however, poisonous and should not be used on toys or kitchen areas.

A further solid constituent of the paint which is generally classified with the pigments is the *extender.* Made from natural white materials such as china clay, mica, silica, barytes, and whiting, the extender when ground to a fine powder becomes transparent in oil and thus has no effect on the colour. However, the various extenders are used to reduce the cost of the paint or improve certain properties such as ease of application, film hardness, and adhesion to undercoats.

c) Additives
Surface coatings are required to perform many specialist functions, and additives are included to fulfil these requirements. Such additives include
  i) catalysts or hardeners, which induce the change from the liquid to the hard surface film (in paints known as two-pack or two-can paints);
 ii) driers, which speed up the drying process;
iii) flatting agents, to reduce the surface gloss;
 iv) thixotropic agents, used in the 'non-drip' paints;
  v) Plasticisers, to prevent the film becoming brittle.

19.2 Application

a) The paint system
This consists of a number of coats applied in sequence to a given surface, and there are a number of factors which must be considered before a system and a particular type of paint are selected. These factors include:
  i) the type of surface to be painted,
 ii) the condition of the surface,
iii) the requirements of the film,
 iv) the finish required,
  v) the colour required,
 vi) the cost.

Oil-bound paints   With these paints, the paint system consists of a primer, undercoat(s), and finishing coat(s). The primer must adhere to the surface at all times and provide a foundation for the subsequent coats. However, in order to ensure that there is adequate adhesion, a certain amount of surface preparation is necessary, especially in the case of old surfaces where existing paint is flaking or rusting has occurred, or on very porous surfaces, where a sealing coat of glue size or other sealer should be applied. In the case of knots in timber, the resin may stain or 'bleed through' the paint system, but aluminium primer can prevent this action or, alternatively, two coats of a special shellac known as 'knotting' can be applied. The colour of the primer should be compatible with the subsequent coats, i.e. a white or light pink primer should be used on joinery where a white or light-coloured final surface finish is required.

After the primer has been applied to a timber surface, any indentations, cracks, or nail holes should be stopped, filled, or smoothed with a proprietary stopper or putty.

Undercoats should adhere to the primer, provide a protective coating, and obliterate the original surface colour. They should also fill up any very small surface depressions and provide a base for the surface coat. The colour of the undercoat should be slightly lighter or darker than that of the final or finishing coat.

The finishing coat provides the final surface texture and colour and is the first line of defence against damage caused by weather, moisture, chemicals, or mechanical means. The gloss and eggshell finishes weather well, without collecting dust and dirt to the same extent as the matt finish.

Water-bound paints   Most of the paint used under this classification is that known as emulsion, but cement paint, the distempers, and lime-wash all come into this category. Emulsions are available in a full range of colours and surface finishes and they can be used externally, but their main use is on large internal surfaces such as walls and ceilings, where two or three coats replace the need for primer, undercoat, and finish.

b) Drying

Most paints should not be applied in humid conditions or when the temperature is less than 4 °C as both conditions slow down the rate of drying, and the moisture present in humid conditions will reduce the film's adhesive properties. The ideal conditions are provided by light good ventilation, without excessive heat, and by using a thin film (0.1 mm thick).

Drying takes place by a combination of one or more of the following:

 i) evaporation,
 ii) oxidation,
 iii) polymerisation,
 iv) coalescence.

If a thick film or excessive heat is applied, the film surface will dry out and harden, leaving a soft weak layer beneath.

With the general exception of emulsion paints, the painting of any surface should be carried out by maintaining a 'wet edge', i.e. the edge of the paint should not be allowed to dry out until the whole area has been completed; thus careful planning is required before a coating is applied (fig. 19.2).

c) Tools

Brushes (fig. 19.3)   There are many types of brush available, their selection depending on the type of paint, the area to be covered, and the location and type of painting to be carried out. Brush widths vary from 12 mm to 100 mm

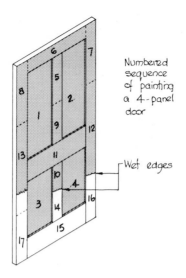

Numbered sequence of painting a 4-panel door

Wet edges

Fig. 19.2 Wet edge

Stock

Ferrule

Setting

Filling

Flat brush

Two-knot Distemper

Flat Distemper (nailed stock)

Stippler

Fig. 19.3 Brushes

in thicknesses from 6 mm to 25 mm, and are made of bristle, hair, nylon, or other synthetic fibres.

Never more than half the filling of the brush should be dipped in the paint and, provided the application is vigorous, the majority of air, dust, and moisture will be removed from the surface. Care should be taken to avoid leaving brush marks on the finished surface, and for quality work a 'worn-in' brush is better than a new one in this respect. Brushes in use can be stored overnight by suspending them in water, but on completion of the work they should be thoroughly cleaned and dried.

Rollers (fig. 19.4)   Rollers are used on large flat or textured surface areas. They have the advantage that the paint is applied several times faster than by a brush and the problem of brush marks is overcome; however, a fine texture called 'orange peel' often results. High surfaces can be reached by the use of a long broom-handle extension, thereby reducing the need for scaffolding. The disadvantages are that the roller cannot paint into angles and is difficult to use on complex work.

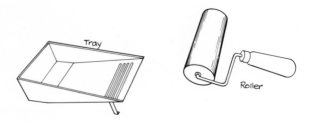

Fig. 19.4 Roller and tray

The roller consists of a handle supporting an axle around which rotates a cylinder 63 mm diameter and 125 to 175 mm long. The cylinder is covered with a sleeve of lambswool, mohair, sponge rubber, plastics foam, or fibre. The lambswool covering holds a good quantity of paint but tends to matt after prolonged use, whereas the mohair probably provides the best finish but is the most expensive.

The paint is held in a shallow tray with a ribbed surface and the roller, having been immersed in the paint, is rolled over the ribs to spread the paint evenly over and through the sleeve. Angles and other difficult areas are usually finished by brush.

Pads   Used in situations where brushes or rollers could be used, with the exception of very small difficult areas, pads have the advantage of being able to be used on angles and with care they produce an even surface finish. The pad consists of a handle attached to a firm base on which is fixed a foam cushion supporting a short-pile mohair or synthetic-fibre face. Pad sizes vary from 50 mm x 25 mm to 150 mm x 75 mm. The pad face is dipped into a tray and worked over a ribbed surface or roller, which again distributes the paint over the whole pad surface before application.

Spray   The spray technique is suitable for large areas or areas having a rough or intricate surface. Very smooth surface finishes can also be achieved. The equipment can be broken down into two components (fig. 19.5):
 i) the pressure equipment,
ii) the gun.

146

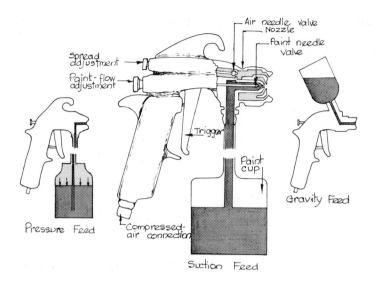

Fig. 19.5 Spray equipment

The pressure equipment can be classified as high or low air pressure (2.7 bar or 0.4 bar), being supplied from a compressor driven by an electric motor or a diesel or petrol engine.

The gun trigger controls the rate of flow of air, or the rate of flow of air and paint, while the nozzle size determines the materials which can be sprayed and the fineness of the spray.

The low-pressure air supply is used in conjunction with a gravity-feed cup fitted on top of a gun, and the high-pressure supply is linked with a suction-type pot under the gun or a pressure pot which feeds the paint to the gun.

In the airless spray, paint is pumped at very high pressure through a very fine orifice, causing rapid expansion on contact with the atmosphere and resulting in a very fine mist effect. The paint may require thinning in order to pass through the orifice.

When applying paint by this method, the surface should be clean and the spraying should be carried out with the gun held at right angles to the surface and between 200 and 300 mm away. The spray is applied with horizontal strokes, each stroke overlapping the previous one by approximately 40% in order to produce an even coating.

20   Hot- and cold-water supply

Understands the principles of hot and cold water installation.

20.1 Describes direct and indirect hot and cold water systems and explains how they function.
20.2 Sketches typical pipework layouts indicating components and controls.
20.3 Describes suitable types of flow controls.
20.4 Describes the purpose of storage cisterns and methods of support.
20.5 Describes the functions and operation of indirect hot water storage cylinders.
20.6 Identifies fittings required for a pipework installation.

Acknowledgement is due to the Technician Education Council for permission to use the content of the TEC units in this chapter. The council reserves the right to amend the content of its units at any time.

20.1 Types of system

a) The direct cold-water system (fig. 20.1)
In this system the incoming water supply from the service pipe is used to supply all cold-water outlets, including sanitary fittings. This system is economical on pipework and requires only a small storage cistern, but it is not generally recommended for two reasons:
 i) in the event of a supply failure there is no cold-water reserve, and, in times of peak demand on the whole supply network, noticeable pressure reductions occur;
ii) syphonage may occur from an appliance, which could lead to a risk of contamination of the mains water.

b) The indirect cold-water system (fig. 20.2)
In this system the incoming water rises directly to the cold-water storage cistern, with only one connection, for drinking-water purposes, being taken from the rising main, usually to the kitchen sink. This system increases the amount of pipework required and the storage capacity of the cistern, but provides a small reserve cold-water supply and reduces the risk of contamination. Since all other sanitary appliances are fed from the cistern, there is generally less pressure on the taps and valves, and therefore less wear.

148

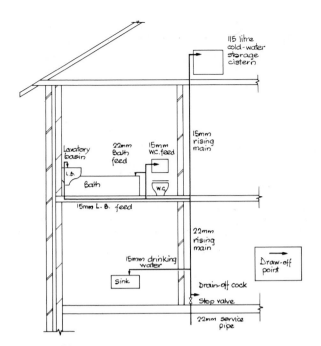

Fig. 20.1 Direct cold-water system

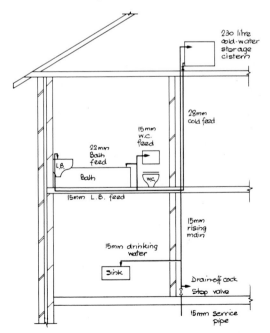

Fig. 20.2 Indirect cold-water system

149

c) The direct hot-water system (fig. 20.3)

In this system, water is taken from the cold-water storage cistern, through the hot-water storage cylinder, and is heated by means of a boiler or back-boiler. The heated water rises by natural convection to the hot-water storage cylinder and is drawn off from the top of the cylinder to the various appliances. In order to prevent air locks and pressure build-up resulting from the expansion of the hot water, an expansion pipe is taken from the top of the cylinder and discharges over the cold-water storage cistern.

The distribution of hot water from the cylinder is usually by a single-pipe system which is non-circulatory, thus requiring the contents of the pipe to be run off before hot water is discharged. This is obviously wasteful, and water authorities may restrict the length of such runs to 12 m for pipes not exceeding 19 mm diameter, 7.5 m for 18 mm diameter, and 3 m for pipes exceeding 35 mm diameter. Where long runs are involved, a secondary circulation is incorporated, the primary circulation being that between the boiler and the cylinder.

A subsidiary means of heating the water is by the inclusion of a 3 kW electric immersion heater in the hot-water cylinder.

d) The indirect hot-water system (fig. 20.4)

In this system, the water is again heated by a boiler but this is not the same water which is drawn off at the taps. A form of heat exchanger is incorporated in the hot-water cylinder and is directly linked in a primary circuit with the boiler. Water in the cylinder surrounds and is heated by the exchanger and is drawn off in the same way as in the direct system. Because there are now two separate hot-water 'circuits', two storage cisterns are required; the second, supplying a primary circuit, does not need to have a large capacity as there should be no draw-off from that section.

This system has a number of advantages:
 i) there is a faster warm up of water because there is continuous circulation without draw-off on the primary side.
 ii) A separate hot-water central-heating system can be incorporated in the primary flow without affecting the temperature of the hot-water run-off.
 iii) In some parts of the country where the cold-water supply is hard, furring of the pipes occurs as a result of lime being precipitated at a temperature of approximately 65 °C. In the direct system, fresh water is supplied to the boiler after each draw-off, causing more precipitation; whereas in the indirect system, once the initial precipitation has occurred, further furring is unlikely.

The selection of a hot-water system is based on a number of factors which include the nature of the water supply (hard or soft), the method of central heating to be used in the property, the ease of installation and maintenance, and the costs involved.

150

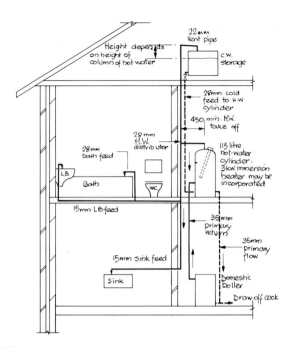

Fig. 20.3 Direct hot-water system

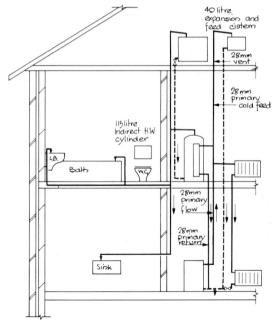

Fig. 20.4 Indirect hot-water system

151

20.2 Typical pipework layouts

Figures 20.1 to 20.4 indicate typical simple pipework layouts, but it should be remembered that the layout must be designed to suit the individual property.

20.3 Flow controls

There are two main types of flow control: (a) taps and (b) valves.

a) Taps

There is a wide variety of taps available, but they fall into the following categories.

i) *Screw-down bib tap* (fig. 20.5)   A piston or jumper with a washer on the end is screwed down on to a seating to restrict the flow. The inlet to the tap is horizontal.

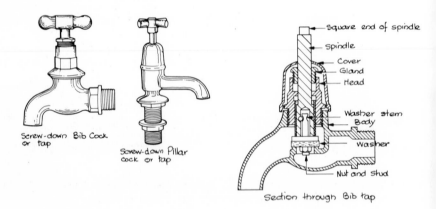

Fig. 20.5 Taps

ii) *Screw-down pillar tap* (fig. 20.5)   Generally used in conjunction with sinks, lavatory basins, and baths, this is similar to (i) but has a vertical inlet. These taps are available in a wide range of materials and can have many forms of control handle.

iii) *Self-closing taps*   These avoid wasting water in institutional or educational buildings. The handle is depressed for the flow to begin and a return spring pushes the head back up when the handle is released, thus shutting off the water.

iv) *Spray taps*   A rose inserted in the outlet of the bib and pillar taps restricts the flow of water, thereby reducing water consumption. Some manufacturers produce a spray tap which also mixes the hot and cold water, so that the user can select the water temperature required. However, for effective operation, the pressure of the hot and the cold water must be equal, which in turn requires the cold-water supply to be from an indirect system.

b) Valves

These isolate a pipeline rather than controlling the flow at the end of a line (fig. 20.6).

i) *Screw-down stop valve* (BS 1010:part 2:1973)   Very similar to the bib tap, (a) (i), but having a horizontal outlet.

ii) *Gate valve* (BS 5154:1974 for copper alloy or BS 5150:1974 and BS 5151: 1974 for cast iron)   Used on larger diameter pipework (38 mm diameter upwards). A wedge-shaped gate is raised within the valve body, but debris may collect in the slide and prevent full shut-off.

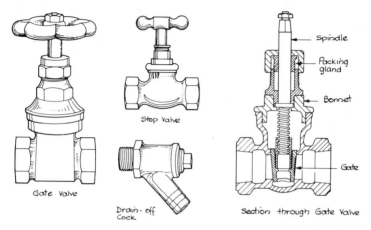

Fig. 20.6 Valves

iii) *Non-return valve*   A gravity or spring-loaded mechanism prevents a return flow, the valve being used to prevent syphonage occurring.

iv) *Mixing valves*   As with the mixer tap, the hot- and cold-water supplies should have an equal pressure. There are two types of valve: the manual and the thermostatic. The manual valves (BS 1415:part 1:1976) are suitable only for kitchens or areas where temperature variation is not critical, the variation resulting from unequal flows within the system. The thermostatic valves are more versatile and can maintain a given temperature to within very fine limits — but are more expensive.

20.4 Storage cisterns (fig. 20.7)

It has already been stated that the storage cistern acts as a small reserve supply of cold water. This supply will prevent overheating of the hot-water system if hot water is drawn off during a failure of the cold-water supply. By having the outlet from the cistern above the bottom, the cistern acts as a sedimentation tank, allowing dirt to settle to the bottom and thus preventing it from entering the hot-water system.

The size of the cistern depends on the number of fittings it supplies. The recommended capacities are 115 litres for cold-water supply only, or 230 litres for both hot- and cold-water supply.

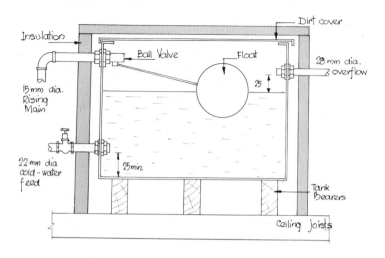

Labels on figure:
- Insulation
- Dirt cover
- Ball Valve
- Float
- 28 mm dia. overflow
- 25
- 15 mm dia. Rising Main
- 22 mm dia cold - water feed
- 25 min.
- Tank Bearers
- Ceiling joists

Fig. 20.7 Water-storage cistern

Cisterns are made of plastics, glass fibre, asbestos, copper, or galvanised mild steel, the latter having only a limited life as a result of the breakdown of the zinc coating. The plastics varieties are flexible — an important factor when access for installation in a loft area is required.

The cold-storage water tank can be positioned in the loft space or immediately above the hot-water cylinder, but the position will influence the pressure of water at the discharge points — a factor which can affect high-level discharges such as showers.

Wherever the cistern is positioned, there must be adequate support since the self weight, contents, and fittings may total as much as 250 kg. If positioned in the loft, it should be set on wooden bearers and not directly on the ceiling joists. It should also be thermally insulated as a protection against frost, and covered to prevent contamination by debris.

Cisterns used in connection with water closets are mentioned in the next chapter.

20.5 The indirect hot-water cylinder

This cylinder can be considered in two parts: the outer cylinder section containing the secondary water and the inner section containing the primary water. The primary water is the water which is heated in the boiler; the secondary water is heated by the primary water, using the high thermal conductivity of the walls of the inner section as a heat exchanger as the water is drawn off for use.

Natural thermal-convection currents in the water are used to operate the system. The boiler-heated water rises to the cylinder and passes into the top of the heat exchanger (a coil of pipe or a corrugated copper cylinder).

As the heat is transferred through the walls of the exchanger, the cooled water returns through the bottom of the exchanger to the boiler for reheating (fig. 20.8). The secondary water, heated by the exchanger, rises to the top of the cylinder and is replaced by cooler water. The hot water draw-off is situated at the top of the cylinder so that, when water is drawn off, it is the hot water which is forced out of the cylinder by the pressure of the cold water entering near the base.

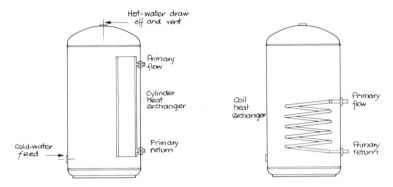

Fig. 20.8 Indirect hot-water cylinders

In order to avoid the need for a cold-water feed cistern and consequent pipework and fittings for the primary circuit, the 'Primatic' cylinder was developed (fig. 20.9). The cylinder is installed in the same manner as a direct cylinder. As the cylinder is filled, so also is the primary system, creating an air seal in the primatic unit. The expansion which takes place when the primary water is heated displaces some of the air in the upper seal into the lower seal. Any excess air in the primary system is automatically vented through the secondary system and, should the water in the primary system require replenishing, this is automatically done from the secondary system.

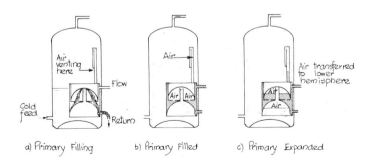

Fig. 20.9 'Primatic' cylinder

155

20.6 Pipework fittings

There are a number of standard fittings available for small-diameter pipework, with various methods of connection (figs. 20.10 and 20.11). They should be made from the same material as the pipes themselves or, if dissimilar, should not cause any problems resulting from electrolytic action.

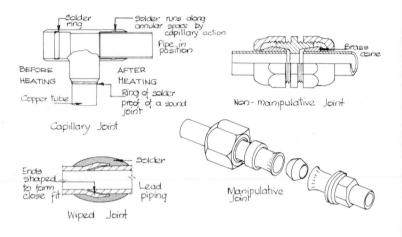

Fig. 20.10 Pipework joints

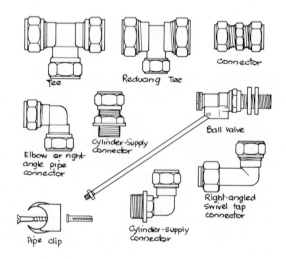

Fig. 20.11 Fittings

21 Sanitation

Understands the principal factors involved in the selection of sanitary fitments and the space required for their installation.

21.1   Identifies the sanitary fitments required for a typical domestic installation.

21.2   Sketches and describes waste and water connections to these fitments.

21.3   Sketches the single-stack system of above-ground drainage and describes its operation.

21.4   Identifies the provisions to be made during construction to accommodate sanitary fitments and services.

Acknowledgement is due to the Technician Education Council for permission to use the content of the TEC units in this chapter. The council reserves the right to amend the content of its units at any time.

21.1 Fitments

Sanitary fitments may be divided into two categories: (a) soil appliances and (b) waste appliances.

a) Soil appliances

Soil appliances are fitments for the collection and discharge of human excreta and other solid matter and include water closets, urinals, and slop sinks. In accordance with the Building Regulations, approved document G, clause 4, they should have a surface which is smooth, non-absorbent, and capable of being easily cleaned, with any flushing apparatus being capable of cleansing the receptacle effectively.

Water-closets (W.C.'s) There are two main types, classified by their cleansing action: the wash-down and the syphonic types (fig. 21.1).

The wash-down type relies on the force and volume of flushing water to wash away and clear the contents of the bowl. It is the cheapest and most popular type, but is noisy in operation.

There are two types of syphonic W.C. — the single trap, in which a restriction of the outlet creates a syphonic action, and the double trap, in which air is drawn from the pipe connecting the two traps, thereby creating syphonage from the bowl. The syphonic action is a more efficient method of cleaning and clearing the bowl, and these forms of W.C. have a quicker action than the wash-down type, but are more expensive.

The fitments are made of earthenware, vitreous china, or stainless steel with the seat and cover of plastics or hardwood. The pedestal unit is fixed

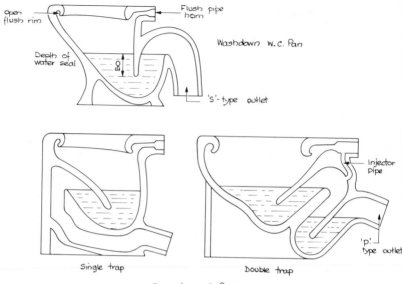

Washdown W.C. Pan

open flush rim

Flush pipe horn

Depth of water seal

'S'-type outlet

Injector pipe

'p' type outlet

Single trap

Double trap

Syphonic W.C. Pans

Fig. 21.1 Water closets

to the floor with brass screws, while the wall-mounted unit is fixed to substantial cantilever wall brackets.

b) Waste appliances

These can be defined as 'appliances for the collection and disposal of water after use for ablutionary, culinary and other domestic purposes' and they include slipper baths, lavatory basins, sinks, bidets, and shower trays (figs 21.2 and 21.3).

i) *Slipper baths*   Manufactured in enamelled cast iron to BS 1189:1972, enamelled sheet steel to BS 1390:1972, and glass fibre or acrylic sheet to BS 4305:1972, this fitment is generally rectangular in shape and is available in a wide range of colours and styles. The basic bath has a flat bottom, with just sufficient fall to the outlet for drainage purposes, and holes for overflow, outlet, and tap connections. Hand grips and rests for soap, sponge, and scrubbing brush may be optional extras. The bath sits on adjustable feet or in a purpose-made cradle, the sides being enclosed by panels made of glass fibre or acrylic, moulded sheets, or enamelled hardboard or plywood, fixed to a timber or metal frame.

ii) *Shower unit*   This may be used in conjunction with the bath or be a separate fitment with a shower tray. The shower tray is manufactured of earthenware or similar materials to those used in manufacturing baths and is available with a central, side, or corner overflow or, if connected to a floor channel, with no overflow at all.

158

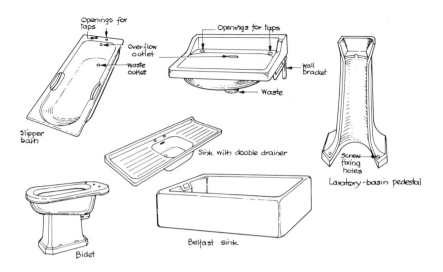

Fig. 21.2 Waste appliances

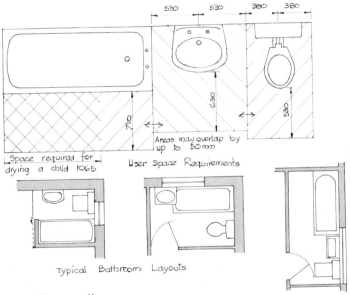

Fig. 21.3 Waste appliances

iii) *Lavatory (wash) basins*   Made of earthenware, steel, or acrylic material, they are supported by a pedestal from the floor, by cantilever wall brackets, or by a combination of the two. The basin can be rectangular on plan for

159

a mid-wall position or quadrant-shaped for a corner mounting. These units are usually manufactured with an integral waste and overflow.

iv) *Sinks*   Similar to lavatory basins but larger, deeper, and generally rectangular in elevation as well as on plan. The shallower London sink is not as popular as the deeper Belfast type. The sink is used for food preparation and washing-up purposes and is fed directly from the cold-water supply. Modern sinks made from enamelled pressed steel or stainless steel have integral draining board(s) and base shelving. The sink is supported by metal or brick legs, cantilever wall brackets, or, in the case of the modern lightweight units, on a purpose-made cupboard unit.

v) *Bidet*   Used primarily for cleansing the excretory organs, this is of similar design to the pedestal W.C. but may be used as a foot bath.

The selection of sanitary units is made on the basis of cost, appearance, durability, cleanliness, and size. The size of a unit is not the only criterion in the layout design, since allowances must be made for the circulation of people using the appliances, as well as their screening.

In any dwelling, the Building Regulations (sections G2 and G4) require the provision of at least one closet and at least one room with a fixed bath or shower. Other building types should have provision in accordance with BS 6465. It is preferable to have a W.C. on both the ground and the first floor; but, if only one W.C. is provided, the bath and W.C. should be separately accommodated and, where this is done, there should be a lavatory basin in the W.C. compartment. It should be emphasised that the latter are only recommendations and the Building Regulations only require plans of new buildings, extensions, and material alterations to show that 'sufficient sanitary conveniences' are to be provided. In the case of situations other than a private dwelling, the numbers of W.C.'s, lavatory basins, etc. required are specifically laid down under various Acts of Parliament.

The Building Regulations (clause G4) require that a space containing a closet or urinal should not open directly into a space used for the preparation of food or where washing up is done, and it should be separated from places where food is stored. In cases where sanitary accomodation opens directly into a bedroom, there should be other sanitary arrangements available within the property for common use. All sanitary accommodation should have vetilation to the external air either by means of an opening light of size not less than one twentieth of the floor area of that accommodation or by a mechanical extractor giving not less than three air changes per hour.

21.2 Connections to fitments

a) Soil appliances

The supply of water to the W.C. is by means of a flushing cistern and flushing pipe (BS 1125:1973) — fig. 21.4. The cistern is manufactured from ceramics, plastics, pressed steel, or cast iron and may be positioned at high or low level or may be integral with the closet itself, in which case no flushing pipe is required. The cold-water supply to the cistern is taken from either the direct

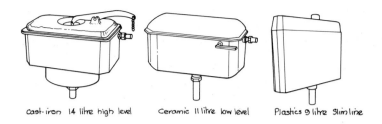

cast-iron 14 litre high level   Ceramic 11 litre low level   Plastics 9 litre Slim line

Fig. 21.4 W.C. cisterns

or indirect supply system and is controlled by means of a ball valve or flushing valve.

There are two main types of ball valve: the 'Croydon' and the more popular 'Portsmouth' (fig. 21.5). Others have been developed to overcome such problems as water hammer and encrustation of moving parts. A quieter refill operation can be achieved by fitting a refill pipe to the valve outlet.

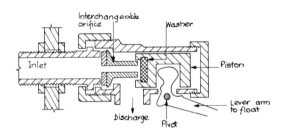

Fig. 21.5 'Portsmouth' ball valve

The flushing valve does away with the need for a cistern, the flow of water through the valve also acting as a self-metering agent. The valve is regulated for a 9, 11, or 14 litre flush, which is the same quantity of water held by the cisterns.

The discharge from the cistern is by syphonic action using a bell syphon or the more common piston type. The cast-iron bell is lifted by a lever and chain; water is also 'lifted' at the same time and is discharged down the flushing pipe, setting up a syphonic action. This type of cistern is durable but noisy and is suitable only for a high-level installation. The piston type lifts the water by means of a cut-away piston supporting a rubber or plastics diaphragm (fig. 21.6).

The cisterns are supported on the wall by heavy-duty brackets. Although the level of water in the cistern is governed by the ball valve, wear on the washers will occur. A 22 mm diameter overflow or warning pipe should be

161

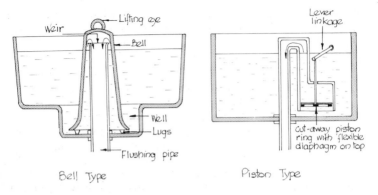

Fig. 21.6 Flushing methods

fitted to discharge outside the building, thus giving a visual warning of washer wear.

The flushing pipe is connected to the cistern by a mechanical joint, while at the lower end the joint between the pipe and the pedestal is made by a rubber or plastics connector (fig. 21.7).

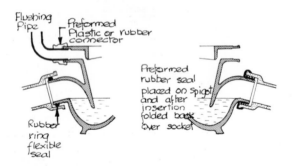

Fig. 21.7 Flushing connections

The outlet from the W.C. is connected to the socket of a soil-pipe using a rigid or flexible joint, and the position of the soil-pipe will vary according to whether the appliance has a 'P' or 'S' trap (fig. 21.8) having a side or back outlet.

b) Waste appliances (fig. 21.9)
The supply of water to lavatory basins, baths, sinks, etc. is regulated by screw-down bib or pillar taps. These fittings are fixed to the appliances by nuts screwed on to the threaded body of the tap. Water is discharged through

a metal, usually chromium-plated, outlet which fits into a preformed hole in the appliance and is again secured by a locknut underneath. The joint between outlet and appliance is sealed with a putty mixture on the inside and with a lead or plastics washer on the outside.

The outlet for a basin will usually incorporate an overflow slot in the body, to collect the discharge from the integral overflow system of the basin, and the outlet is connected to a trap. The trap prevents foul gases from the drainage system entering the property and also prevents large or heavy articles, which might cause a blockage, being discharged into the drains. Approved document H of the Building Regulations requires all points of discharge of a sanitary system to have a water-sealed trap, with a minimum depth of seal of 75 mm (except a W.C., where a minimum 50 mm depth of seal is required). The traps are made of copper or copper alloy (BS 1184:1976) or plastics (BS 3943:1979), having a 'P' or 'S' outlet and incorporating a cleaning eye. A modern alternative to the 'P' or 'S' trap is the high-density-polythene bottle trap (fig 21.8). Older premises may still have traps formed in lead.

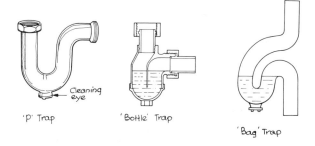

Fig. 21.8 Traps

It is usual to provide an overflow to a waste appliance. Such an overflow should 'discharge into a waste-pipe in such a way as to be disconnected from the drainage system, or so discharge as not to cause dampness in, or damage to any part of any building'. In the case of sinks and basins, the overflow is generally incorporated in the appliance, while the overflow for a bath may discharge outside the building or by means of a flexible tube connected to the outlet.

21.3 The single-stack system
In the 1950's, more economic methods of construction were being investigated, and the Building Research Station experimented with a single vertical pipe — called a stack — for carrying both soil and waste water from the respective appliances to the underground system, without the need for ventilating pipes.

These ventilating pipes were previously required to prevent the loss of the water seal in traps by pressure variations in the stack(s) (fig. 21.11). These pressure variations are caused by

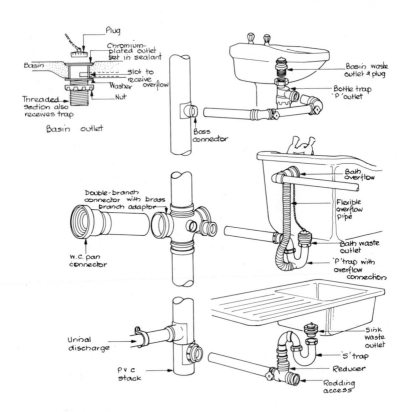

Fig. 21.9 Waste-appliance connections

a) *induced syphonage* —the flow of water down a stack causes suction in the waste-pipe from an appliance drawing water from the trap;

b) *back pressure* — the flow of water down a stack, especially in the vicinity of a sharp bend near the foot of a stack, may cause an increase in pressure in the waste-pipe from an appliance, forcing foul air through the trap and into the room (fig. 21.10);

c) *self syphonage* — the flow of waste water from an appliance, running full in the waste-pipe, may cause suction in the pipe which will draw water from the trap.

The effects of (a) and (c) can be overcome either by preventing the suction occurring — the old method — or by paying close attention to design detail. Approved document H of the Building Regulations gives design criteria for branch discharge pipes, their positioning and connection to the stack (fig. 21.12), and stack sizing.

The effect of (b) is overcome by not allowing connections to the stack at specific points and by increasing the radius of the bend at the foot of the stack.

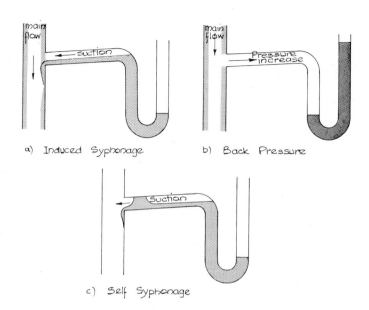

a) Induced Syphonage   b) Back Pressure

c) Self Syphonage

Fig. 21.10 Stack pressure problems

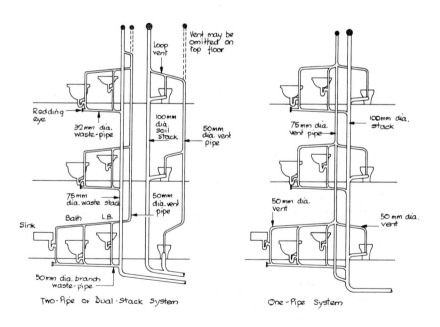

Two-Pipe or Dual-Stack System

One-Pipe System

Fig. 21.11 One-pipe and two-pipe systems

165

The stack should be open to the air at the top, but protected by a balloon wire grating, thus allowing ventilation of the drainage system. It must have a minimum diameter of 75 mm (100 mm is more usual) and be composed of suitable materials, usually plastics or cast iron. The stack can be placed outside the building, provided that the building has not more than three storeys or was built prior to the 1976 Building Regulations coming into operation. The main design features are shown in fig. 21.12.

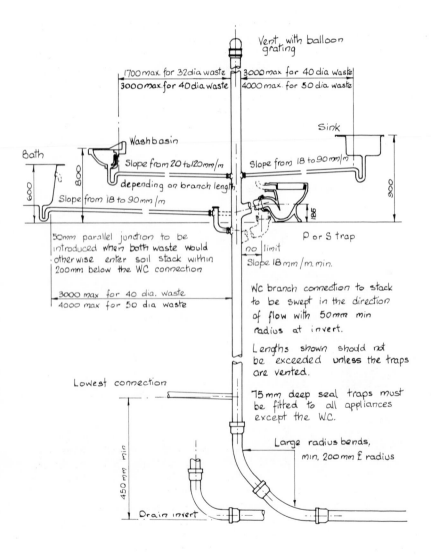

Fig. 21.12 Single-stack drainage

21.4 Provision for sanitation

The sanitary fitments themselves are usually installed during the second or final fixing carried out by the plumber. In the first fixing the soil-stack is temporarily positioned, especially if it is situated inside the property, so that flooring and a timber-frame casing can be constructed around it. Hot- and cold-water service runs are also installed if they are to be run in ducts, in or through walls, or in the floor screed or space in the case of a suspended timber floor, the runs being temporarily capped or closed off to prevent entry of debris or vermin.

The connection for joining the stack to the drainage system is laid under or through the foundations during the construction of the substructure, and is terminated with a socket end just above the ground-floor or footpath level. This connection should be sealed with a temporary stopper until the soil-stack is positioned, in order to prevent debris entering the drain. The full height of the stack is erected, so that roof coverings and flashings can be fitted around the stack where it projects through a roof.

There should be adequate support for all water- and waste-pipes. This is provided by wall-mounted fixing clips (fig. 21.13) which not only hold the pipework in position, but, in the case of copper water-pipes, also prevent pipes from coming into contact with 'cold' external walls. All the service pipework must also be able to accommodate thermal movement.

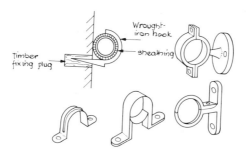

Fig. 21.13 Pipework support

Holes through an external wall, which may be required for the connection of soil- and waste-pipes to an externally located stack, may be left out during construction, but it is more usual for these to be broken out as and when the plumber is making the connection at the second fixing stage.

In the case of a ground-floor waste appliance, there is no need for it to be connected to the stack provided that it discharges into an external back inlet gulley, the connection being made either through the external wall above ground level or through the substructure (fig. 21.14). In the latter case, a special reducing adaptor is available.

167

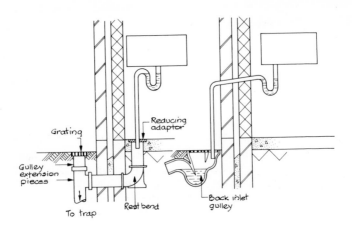

Fig. 21.14 Back inlet gulley

168

22   Drainage

Understands the principles of constructing simple drainage systems incorporating inspection chambers.

22.1 *Distinguishes between 'separate' and 'combined' drainage systems.*
22.2 *Draws annotated line diagrams of these systems.*
22.3 *States purpose of highway drains.*
22.4 *Defines and states purpose of:*
    subsoil,
    carrier,
    cut off,
    French drains,
    open ditches.
22.5 *Sketches and describes the construction of a typical highway drainage system to a river outfall.*
22.6 *Sketches and describes methods of laying rigid and flexible drains.*

Acknowledgement is due to the Technician Education Council for permission to use the content of the TEC units in this chapter. The council reserves the right to amend the content of its units at any time.

22.1 Separate and combined drainage systems
In Volume 1, section 16.4, a separate sewerage system was defined as being 'two separate drainage systems, one carrying foul or soil water to the sewage-purification works, the other carrying rain-water to discharge directly into a watercourse or the sea'; the combined sewerage system as 'waste water from both rain-water and soil fittings conveyed in one sewer to the sewage-treatment works'.

The separate system is more expensive to install since two pipelines must be laid, each having its own ancillary fittings such as manholes. However, in the long term the overall cost of the system is cheaper, as there is a more or less constant flow of foul water to the sewage-treatment works, thereby enabling economic treatment of the sewage to be carried out.

The combined system is cheaper to install as only one pipe, albeit of larger diameter, is laid; however, fluctuating flows and concentrations of sewage at the treatment works require not only a larger works but also more expensive forms of treatment.

22.2 Typical systems
The plans shown in fig. 22.1 indicate typical layouts for a site using (i) the separate system and (ii) the combined system.

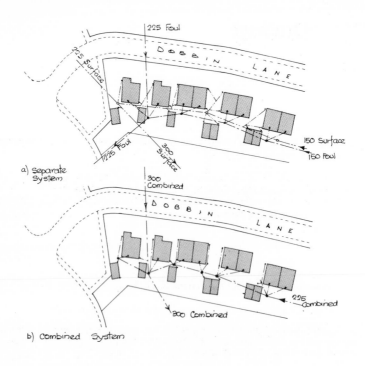

Fig. 22.1 Separate and combined drainage systems

22.3 Highway drains (fig. 22.2)

These remove the rain-water falling solely on the highway, and they may eventually discharge into a combined or surface-water sewer. They are designed to carry away a given volume of rainfall which has been statistically calculated to occur once in a given number of years (e.g. 75 mm/h with a probability of occurrence once every 20 years). To design the drainage for a greater intensity would be uneconomic.

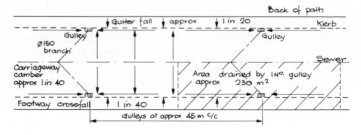

Fig. 22.2 Highway drainage

22.4 Definitions

a) *Subsoil drainage* removes or lowers ground water and subsoil water from the ground in the vicinity of the drain, and is carried out for a number of reasons:

    i) to dry out areas of the subsoil which would otherwise have a high moisture content and therefore a lower load-bearing capacity;

    ii) to drain water from the surface of the ground, which would otherwise remain in the form of ponds or marshes;

    iii) to improve the angle of repose of the soil in cuttings or embankments, so that less land is required for construction purposes;

    iv) to reduce the hydrostatic pressure on basements;

    v) to improve the workability of soil for agricultural purposes.

There are a number of layout patterns which are used depending on the site circumstances, and they are the natural, herring-bone, fan, and grid patterns (fig. 22.3).

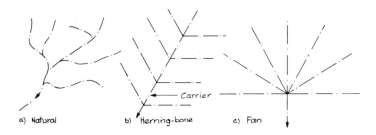

a) Natural   b) Herring-bone   c) Fan

Fig. 22.3 Subsoil drainage patterns

The subsoil drains are laid in narrow trenches or by means of a mole plough (fig. 22.4) at depths varying between 0.5 m and 1.0 m. The pipes may be porous, partially or fully perforated, or non-porous, and they are manufactured from clayware, concrete, pitch fibre, or plastics, having socket-and-spigot or butt joints. Where the drains pass close to trees or hedges, they should be fully

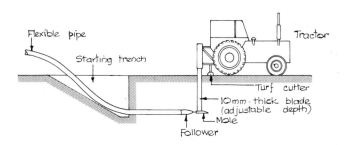

Fig. 22.4 Mole plough

171

jointed in order to prevent the penetration of tree roots. Prior to backfilling, the drains are surrounded by granular material and covered with filter medium such as straw, in order to prevent silting.

b) Except for the fan layout, the branches of the subsoil drain connect with the main drain or *carrier*. The carrier may itself collect water or may be designed to transfer the water from the branches to some discharge point such as a catch-pit.

c) The *cut-off drain*, or moat, is laid on one or more sides of a property in order to intercept the subsoil water and prevent damage to the natural and artificial foundations of the property.

d) *A French drain* (fig. 22.5) is one in which the excavated trench is back-filled with clinker, rubble, or other porous granular material to ground level. There may or may not be pipes laid in the bottom of the trench. This type of drain will take away not only subsoil water but also ground and surface water.

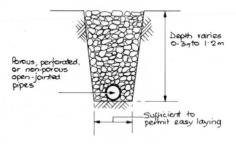

Fig. 22.5 French drain

e) *Open ditches* form a freeway for subsoil and surface water to drain into, but the run-off into them is slower than with the drainage methods previously described. They can also serve as a barrier element in addition to or replacing hedges and fences, as well as acting as a distributor of water in times of drought.

22.5 Highway drainage systems
The layout of a highway drainage system, as with a foul drainage system, is generally dependent upon the topography of the ground (fig. 22.6). The drainage system must be able to carry the unwanted water to the point of discharge at a convenient velocity, using natural falls on the pipe runs, so that too great a depth of excavation is not required during construction.

The construction of a system can be considered in a number of sections.

a) *Excavation* The excavation work is carried out in a trench with suitable timbering incorporated (see section 4.3), the profiles having been established to provide accurate information for both positional and depth requirements (see section 22.6).

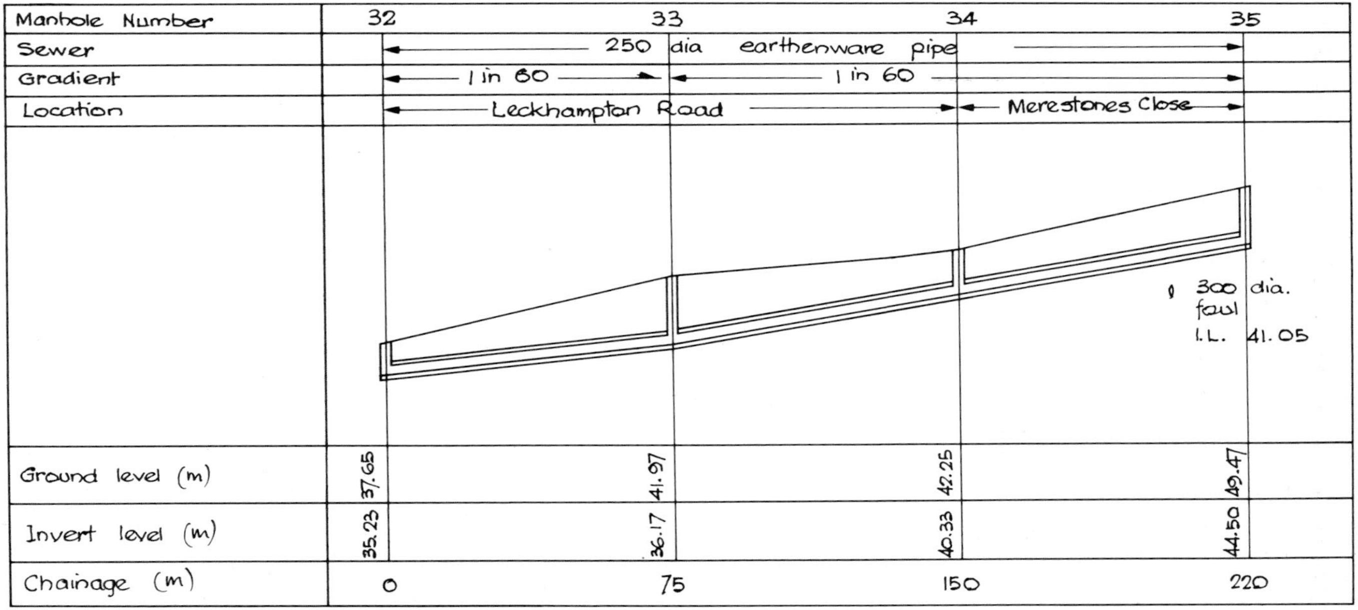

Manhole Number	32	33	34	35
Sewer		250 dia	earthenware pipe	
Gradient	1 in 60	1 in 60	1 in 60	
Location	Leckhampton Road		Merestones Close	

300 dia.
foul
I.L. 41.05

Ground level (m)	37.65	41.97	42.25	49.47
Invert level (m)	35.23	36.17	40.33	44.50
Chainage (m)	0	75	150	220

Section of Proposed Surface Water Sewer at Newtown

Scales - Vertical 1 : 150   Horizontal 1 : 1250

Fig. 22.6 Highway drainage scheme

173

b) *Laying* The main sewer and branches are laid to designed falls, the branches being left open-ended to receive the gulley connections.

c) *Reinstatement* The work being mainly in highways, the reinstatement must be able to stand up to the highway loadings. In the case of a new carriageway construction there is no problem since the sub-base and base will not have been constructed when the sewer is laid. In the case of an existing carriageway it is usual to have controlled backfilling followed by a temporary tar-macadam surface. (The traffic is also allowed to participate in the consolidation process.) Once settlement of the backfill has ceased, the permanent surface reinstatement is carried out.

d) *Gulleys* Road gulleys (fig. 22.7) are set close to the kerb, their exact location depending on the form of grating to be used. The top surface of the gulley is kept some 300 mm below the finished gutter level to allow for the grating and a number of courses of engineering brick (generally two) to make up the level. This brickwork provides a facility for both level and positional adjustment, as well as converting the round plan shape of the gulley top to the rectangular shape of the grating frame. The gulley is set on and surrounded by a 150 mm minimum thickness of concrete. The surround should also be placed around the connecting branch where it is less than 750 mm below the road surface.

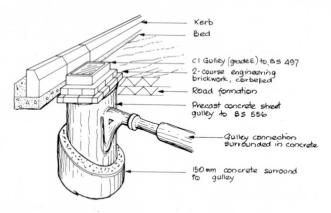

Fig. 22.7 Road gulley

e) *Manholes* In the main, the sewer will be adopted by the local authority (unless the work has already been commissioned by such authority), thus the standard of workmanship will have to be acceptable to the authority. The majority of the manholes constructed in modern highways are formed using circular precast concrete rings which are slotted on top of one another (see Volume 1, fig. 16.13) and are manufactured to BS 5911:part 1:1981, while the cover and frame are in accordance with BS 497:part 1:1976.

f) *Outfall* (fig. 22.8) Where the outfall is at a river or stream, the selection of its siting must be carefully made since there must be

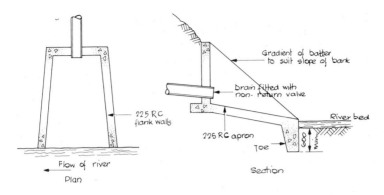

Fig. 22.8 Outfall construction

    i) minimum erosion of the stream bed,
   ii) minimum scour of either bank,
  iii) no movement of the outfall works by settlement,
  iv) no flow of water from the stream into the sewer.

  i) To prevent erosion, the base of the outfall is formed by a reinforced-concrete slab, and the stream bed may either be concreted or have hardcore embedded in it.

 ii) Scour on the discharge banking is prevented by the use of concrete or brick wing walls, while the opposite banking is protected by the roughness of the river bed.

iii) Provision of a slab and toe, provided that they are of sufficient size, will prevent settlement – the major problem being a leakage or seepage of water behind the outfall works.

iv) The invert of the sewer, where it discharges, should be above the anticipated top water level of the stream, but, where sewer gradients make this not possible, a non-return flap valve should be incorporated in the end of the pipe.

It must be noted that, where a new drainage system is to discharge into a watercourse, not only must the work be approved by the local highway authority but also certain of the proposals, concerning volume of discharge and outfall works, must be approved by the regional water authority.

22.6 Drain laying

a) Rigid drains
In excavating for drains, the trench (fig. 22.9) should never be opened up too far in advance of the pipe laying and should be backfilled as soon as possible afterwards. This reduces the risk of accidents, damage to pipes by falls in the trench, flooding, and unnecessary obstruction of the site. The width of the trench at the bottom should be at least 300 mm greater than

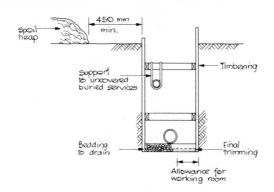

Fig. 22.9 Drain trench

the diameter of the pipes being laid, to allow for working room, and the excavated material should be deposited at least $\frac{1}{2}$ m away from the sides of the trench. Any services uncovered during the excavation work should be adequately supported and protected.

The initial depth of excavation should be some 50 to 75 mm above the final level required – this allows for a final trimming which will provide a firm bed for the barrel of the pipes to rest on. In poor ground conditions, allowances must be made for provision of a concrete bedding.

When laying the drain (fig. 22.10), each pipe is set individually for line and level using line and boning rods, starting from the lower end and ensuring that the barrel of each pipe rests on a firm and even bed and the sockets face uphill. Hand holes must be excavated to receive the individual sockets and allow for jointing.

In the jointing of both clayware and cast- or spun-iron pipes, the gasket (tarred hemp or hemp dipped in grout) is wrapped around the spigot of each pipe before it is placed in the socket, and is caulked home afterwards; this prevents mortar getting into the pipes, as well as assisting in centring the spigot in the socket so that an even bore is achieved. In the case of clayware drains, a 1:1 cement–sand mortar is used to fill the socket and form a fillet – the fillet being trowelled smooth. Except in frosty weather, the joint should be protected with damp sacking to prevent the joint drying out too rapidly and cracking. The joints between iron pipes are made by molten lead being run into the socket and by a jointing ring placed around the barrel against the face of the socket. When the lead is cool, it is caulked tightly home to make up for shrinkage. An alternative to the run-lead joint is that using lead wool, again caulked tightly home (fig. 22.11).

After the drain run has been tested, the backfilling can be carried out. The initial layer around the pipes, and for a minimum of 300 mm above the pipes, should be of selected material, containing no large or hard lumps, which can be easily hand rammed. It should be evenly placed so that equal pressures on either side of the pipeline are maintained. Subsequent backfilling

176

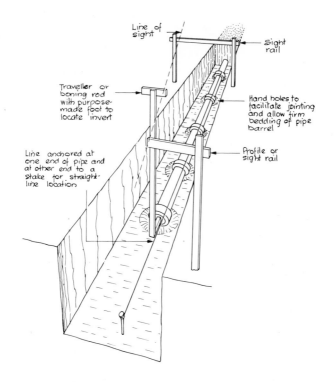

Fig. 22.10 Drain laying

Fig. 22.11 Rigid joints

is carried out in layers approximately 150 mm thick using the excavated material, each layer being well consolidated. A mechanical rammer should be used only once a 1 m depth of fill above the pipes has been reached. Careless backfilling will cause a fractured pipeline either immediately or as a result of subsequent imposed loading.

Where a concrete haunching or surround is required, the concreting should be done in one operation. Once the concrete has set, care is still required in the backfilling procedure.

b) Flexible drains

These may be constructed using rigid pipes with flexible joints or the 'flexible' pipes made of p.v.c. or similar materials. In either case, the same general criteria apply as for the laying of the rigid drains, but with certain exceptions as follows.

The depth of excavation should be at least 100 m deeper than the level to which the drain is to be laid, to allow for a suitable bedding material. This bedding material may be 'as dug', provided the particle size and compaction quality are suitable. Alternatively, a 5 to 10 mm-size gravel or broken stone should be used, provided that it is not chalk or, in acidic ground-water conditions, limestone. Clay should never be used for bedding, as it will never compact sufficiently and is also liable to swell. Hard spots on the bottom of the trench should be removed before compaction of the bedding.

The pipes should be jointed in accordance with the manufacturer's instructions (fig. 22.12), but it is essential in all cases to ensure that the pipes and sealing components are thoroughly clean. Depressions in the bedding will be required to receive sockets, thus ensuring that the barrel of the pipe is adequately supported.

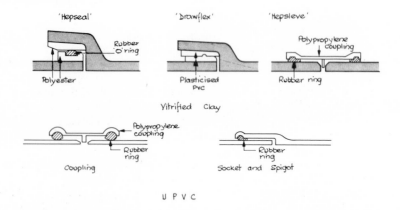

Fig. 22.12 Flexible joints

After the pipe run has been tested, filling around the sides of the pipe should be done in 100 mm layers using the same material as that used for the bedding. The same material may also be used for the next 300 mm of backfill (in 150 mm layers) or, alternatively, pebble-free ballast or clean sand or sandy soil may be used. Subsequent backfilling is carried out using excavated material in layers not exceeding 300 mm.

Concreting around flexible drains is seldom carried out, since a rigid pipeline results. However, the Building Regulations require a concrete surround in certain situations (see Volume 1, fig. 16.7).

178

23   Footways

Understands the construction of footways and the application of surface finishings to footways and pavements.

23.1   Sketches and describes the construction of coated macadam-surfaced footways.
23.2   Sketches and describes the construction of present concrete footways.
23.3   States function of surface dressings on pavement construction.
23.4   Lists materials used for surface dressings, states their characteristics and describes process of application.

Acknowledgement is due to the Technician Education Council for permission to use the content of the TEC units in this chapter. The council reserves the right to amend the content of its units at any time.

A footway is that part of the road which is preserved for pedestrians — as opposed to a footpath, which is a way for pedestrians which is not associated with a road.

The construction of a carriageway and a footway are linked at the kerb (unless there is a verge between them). The kerb serves a number of purposes:
a) it contains the carriageway construction — especially flexible pavements;
b) it contains the footway construction;
c) it acts as a guide, directing the surface water run off;
d) when set out accurately, it acts as a reference for all other highway construction;
e) it also to a large extent contains the heavy traffic on the area designed for it, rather than allowing it on the lighter-constructed footways, thereby preventing damage.

The relationship of the kerb construction to the footway and carriageway construction and kerb terminology are shown in fig. 23.1.

The footway should be designed taking into account the amount and nature of use, the effects of the weather on the surface and users, the appearance, the method of drainage, and the costs involved.

23.1 Macadam footways
There are three types of macadam footways: tar macadam, tar-paving, and bitumen macadam.

a) Tar macadam   The material is composed of
 i) *coarse aggregate* — gravel, crushed rock, or blast-furnace slag;

179

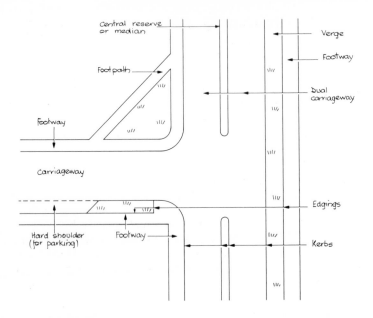

Fig. 23.1 Footway terminology

ii) *fine aggregate* – crushed rock or clean sand, 75% of which will pass a number 200 BS sieve;

iii) *filler* (optional) – limestone, Portland cement, or hydrated lime;

iv) *binder* – tar to BS 76:1974, or a tar/bitumen mixture.

b) Tar-paving   Tar macadam manufactured especially for footpaths and playgrounds, tar-paving is laid in two coats, the base coat having an aggregate of 25 mm nominal size and the wearing coat having a 10 mm aggregate, both being bound by tar to BS 76:1974.

c) Bitumen macadam   Similar to tar macadam but bound by bitumen to BS 3690:1970. Coloured varieties of this material are available.

The construction of a macadam footway consists of a sub-base, a base course, and a wearing course, although in certain instances the base course and wearing course are constructed as one (fig. 23.2). After excavation to formation level and ensuring that adequate subsoil drainage is available, a sub-base of clinker, broken brick, or stone hardcore is spread, levelled, and rolled with a 0.5 tonne vibratory or 2.5 tonne tandem roller to a compacted thickness of 100 mm and to the correct profiles. There should be a minimum cross-fall of 1 in 48.

The base course, consisting of 19 mm or 25 mm aggregate, is laid to a consolidated depth of approximately 40 mm, and the wearing course is

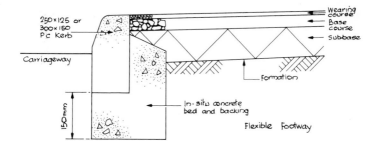

Fig. 23.2 Footway construction

applied immediately after rolling the base course, to a depth of approximately 13 mm using 6 to 10 mm aggregate. The roller used for this operation should be no heavier than that used on the sub-base. Care should be taken around manhole covers and other obstructions, and in such places hand tamping is acceptable.

23.2 Concrete footways
Concrete footways are mainly constructed using rectangular precast concrete flags, but occasionally in-situ concrete is used.

a) *Precast flags* Manufactured to BS 368:1971, the flags are cast and hydraulically pressed in a range of sizes varying from 600 mm x 400 mm to 600 mm x 900 mm and in 50 and 63 mm thicknesses. Coloured flags can also be obtained to provide decoration or to emphasise a particular use at road crossings.

The flags should be laid on a well consolidated granular bed (usually ashes) 100 mm thick and bedded on at least five lime–sand mortar spots to each flag (fig. 23.3). The fall on the footway should be a minimum of 1 in 24, usually towards the kerb, with the flags being laid broken jointed.

The thinner flags are used in most situations except where traffic may occasionally run on the footway, in which case there is less chance of

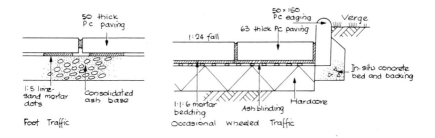

Fig. 23.3 Flagging

the unreinforced flag cracking under the load if the thicker variety is used. Where traffic is likely to run over the footway at frequent intervals, such as at access to garages or drives, the flags should be laid on a green 100 mm in-situ concrete bed which in turn is laid on the consolidated sub-base of ashes.

Since the flags are rigid rather than flexible, certain problems can arise where differing cross-falls meet. In such cases, as well as in situations where the footway is curved on plan, a certain amount of cutting and mitring will be required.

After laying, the joints between flags should be grouted with a cement—sand mortar brushed well in. On completion, any excess mortar should be cleaned off.

b) *In-situ concrete*   Where steep slopes are required for a footway, or where there may be a large amount of cutting of precast flags, a 75 to 100 mm-thick in-situ paving is laid on a plastics or building-paper membrane on a 100 mm consolidated granular base (fig. 23.4). The surface of the concrete is trowelled smooth or, in the case of a steep slope, is left with a tamped finish providing a slip-resistant surface.

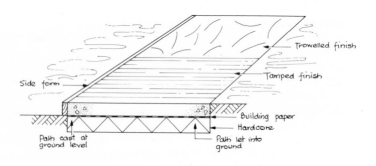

Fig. 23.4 In-situ concrete footway

23.3 Surface dressing
A surface dressing provides the final wearing surface to the wearing course, and the dressing may be provided in order to
a) improve the rate of run-off of rain from the footway — water may be retained for a long period of time in an open-textured wearing course, especially one having no fillers, therefore sealing the surface may improve the durability of the footway;
b) improve slip resistance — a smooth rolled surface may have a poor slip or skid resistance, therefore the addition of a surface dressing may improve this property;
c) provide decoration — colouring a surface may highlight various special areas or just generally improve an otherwise drab footscape.

23.4 Dressing materials

a) *Fine cold asphalt*   This consists of natural aggregate, a binder of bitumen or bitumen with flux, and additives or fillers as required.

When applied to a fresh-coated macadam base, no preparation is needed; but for worn bituminous surfaces, concrete, stone, etc. a tack coat is required. The tack coat should be a labile emulsion which is sprayed evenly over the surface to be coated.

The asphalt should be delivered to the site at a minimum temperature of 15 °C and be deposited in heaps on a clean hard surface. It is then spread by shovels or forks to give a loose uniform layer approximately twice the thickness of the compacted thickness. Compaction to a finished thickness of 13 to 20 mm is achieved by means of a 0.75 to 5 tonne roller.

b) *Hot-rolled asphalt*   This produces a harder more even surface for footways; but, in order to avoid problems of slip, a dusting of grit should be applied. Alternatively, 10 mm coated chippings can be spread at a rate of 4 to 8 kg/m^2 and rolled into the surface.

c) *Grit*   This comprises 5 mm to dust natural aggregate which is rolled into the surface of a new tar-macadam or asphalt footway.

d) *Bituminous grit*   This is applied by hand or mechanically to new open-textured macadam surfaces as a blinding. The materials should comply with tables 53 and 56 in BS 4987:1973.

24   Landscaping

Understands the need for reinstatement, landscaping and the incorporation of street furniture.

24.1   *Lists activities involved in reinstatement and landscaping.*
24.2   *Classifies street furniture as lighting and traffic signs.*
24.3   *Identifies traffic signs as regulatory, informatory and safety.*
24.4   *Describes typical methods of erecting posts and columns.*
24.5   *Draws typical cross and longitudinal highway sections showing location of under- and overground equipment.*

Acknowledgement is due to the Technician Education Council for permission to use the content of the TEC units in this chapter. The council reserves the right to amend the content of its units at any time.

24.1 Activities

Reinstatement is the replacing or restoring of a site to the condition in which it was before work began. Landscaping is the attempt to improve the visual amenity of a site. The various activities can be listed as follows.

a) *Reinstatement*
 i) Backfilling trenches.
 ii) Replacing the surface, e.g. topsoil, turf, crops, pavings, road construction, etc.
 iii) Repairing or replacing damaged fences and hedges.
 iv) Replanting bushes, shrubs, etc. dug up during the site-clearance operation.
 v) Removal of temporary works, such as temporary access roads, cabins, etc.

b) *Soft landscaping*
 i) Forming the ground into interesting visual shape.
 ii) Preparing and topping of the ground.
 iii) Providing subsoil drainage.
 iv) Applying a covering of turf or grass seed.
 v) Planting flower beds.
 vi) Planting shrubs and hedges.
 vii) Planting trees.

c) *Hard landscaping*
 i) Constructing walls.
 ii) Erecting fences.
 iii) Constructing footpaths.
 iv) Providing tree protection.
 v) Installation of playground equipment.
 vi) Provision of outdoor seating and litter receptacles.

24.2 Street furniture

The two major classes of street furniture are (a) street lighting and (b) traffic signs. There is, however, other 'furniture' which does not fall into these categories and can be classified as 'sundries'.

a) Street lighting (fig. 24.1)   This generally comprises a column supporting a lamp.

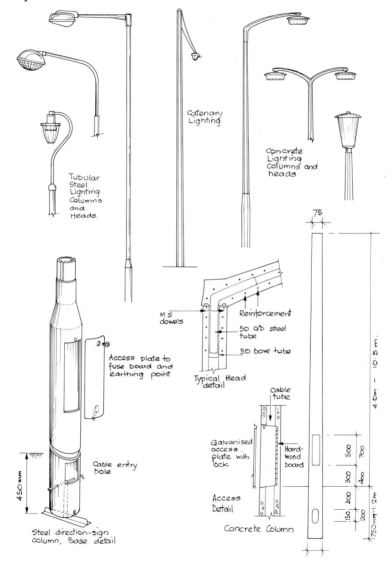

Catenary Lighting

Tubular Steel Lighting Columns and Heads.

Concrete Lighting Columns and heads

M S dowels

Reinforcement

50 o/d steel tube

50 bore tube

Typical Head detail

Access plate to fuse board and earthing point

Cable entry hole

Cable tube

Galvanised access plate with lock

Hard-wood board

Access Detail

Concrete Column

Steel direction-sign column, Base detail

Fig. 24.1 Street lighting

i) *Columns*   The column is manufactured of steel or prestressed concrete and tapers towards its upper end. The length of the column above ground varies from approximately 4 m for side streets and pedestrian ways to over 10 m for main roads, while the length below ground varies from approximately 760 mm to 1.5 m respectively.

    The column has a hole below ground to allow entry of the electricity cable, and an access door some 600 mm above ground to allow access to electricity connections, time switches, etc.

ii) *Brackets*   A wide variety of brackets which support the lantern are available for connection to the top of the column. Their selection will depend on the class of road or footpath, the lighting requirements, and the position of the column relative to those requirements. In certain circumstances the lantern may be suspended on a catenary cable between two columns.

iii) *Lantern*   The selection of a lantern also depends on the situation of the lighting as well as the type of lamp, i.e. mercury or sodium discharge, fluorescent, or filament.

b) Traffic signs   See section 24.3.

c) Sundries (fig. 24.2)   These include
  i) *Bus shelters*
  ii) *Bus-stop signs*

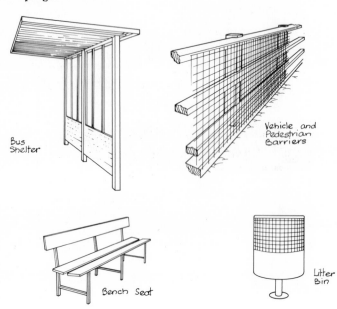

Fig. 24.2 Sundry street furniture

iii) *Pedestrian barriers and guard rails*
iv) *Litter bins*
 v) *Seating*
vi) *Traffic-signal control boxes.*

24.3 Traffic signs (fig. 24.3)
Traffic signs may be classified into the following categories.

a) Regulatory
These signs are mainly concerned with traffic circulation. They should, on the
whole, be externally or internally illuminated if they are erected within 50 m
of a street lamp; otherwise they should be reflectorised.
i) *Compulsory*   These give instructions to drivers about what they must do.
   They are generally circular with white symbols on a blue background,
   but the 'stop' and 'give way' signs are white, red, and black and are shaped
   as shown below.

a) (i) Compulsory

a) (ii) Prohibitory

b) (i) Facilities

c) Warning Signs

Fig. 24.3 Traffic signs

187

ii) *Prohibitory*   These give instructions to drivers about what they must not do. These signs are generally circular with a red border.

b) *Informatory*
 i) *Facilities*   Generally rectangular, consisting of various shapes and colour combinations, but mainly white lettering on a blue background.
ii) *Names*   These give the names of streets, towns, rivers, etc., and the signs are rectangular with various colours of lettering and background.

Warning signs
These signs warn traffic of danger or potential danger ahead. With few exceptions, all safety or warning signs, when erected within 50 m of a street lamp, must be directly illuminated. If not illuminated they must be reflectorised.

The majority of these signs are triangular and contain a black symbol on a white background inside a red border.

d) *Directional* (fig. 24.4)
 i) *Advance directional signs* — give the driver information about the route ahead before he reaches the road junction.
ii) *Direction signs* — give route information at the junction.

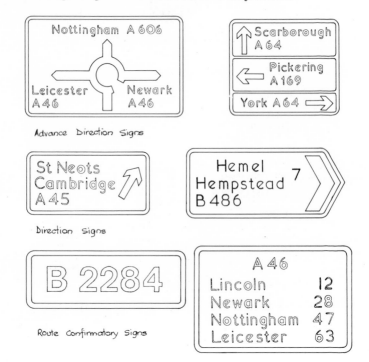

Fig. 24.4 Traffic signs (directional)

iii) *Route confirmatory signs* – give confirmation and additional information
about the route after the junction.

Motorway signs have white lettering and a white border on a blue background. Primary routes have white lettering on a green background with yellow
route numbers. Other direction signs have black lettering on a white background;
and the local direction signs have a blue border.

24.4 Post and column erection

The foundations for any steel furniture should be designed and placed at
such a depth as to carry the posts, columns, lamps, and signs safely without
affecting the surrounding soil. For a small single-post sign, bedding the
tubular post in concrete may well be adequate, whereas for a larger multi-
head street light a special base-plate with holding-down bolts, bedded in a
specially designed concrete pad, may be required (fig. 24.5).

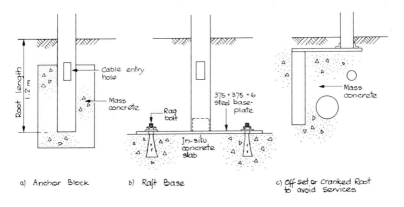

Fig. 24.5 Lighting-column erection

24.5 Cross-sections

Typical highway sections are shown in figs 24.6 and 24.7.

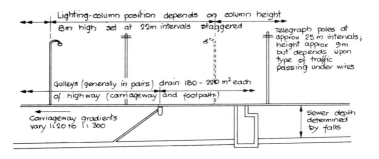

Fig. 24.6 Highway longitudinal section

189

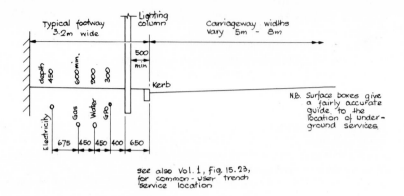

Fig. 24.7 Highway cross-section

25   Bridges

Understands the construction of simple small-span bridges.

25.1   *States performance requirements for small-span bridges including loading and protection from traffic and weather.*
25.2   *Identifies structural components of above and states their functions.*
25.3   *Sketches and describes construction.*

Acknowledgement is due to the Technician Education Council for permission to use the content of the TEC units in this chapter. The council reserves the right to amend the content of its units at any time.

Bridges are designed to facilitate the safe crossing of pedestrians and vehicles over natural and man-made obstacles such as rivers, valleys, roads, canals and railways.

The earliest forms of bridges were the fallen log placed over a stream at a convenient point and the positioning of flat stone slabs on what may have previously been stepping stones (known as a clapper bridge). Both forms embody the simple beam principle.

Both the Greeks and the Romans were well aware of the arch principle and used it in the construction of their bridges. This principle remained the

A brick and stone bridge

basis of bridge construction until the industrial revolution, when the more modern materials of steel and concrete became available. These materials, together with a better understanding of structural design principles, provided engineers with a more economic method of spanning larger distances using suspension and frame techniques (fig. 25.1).

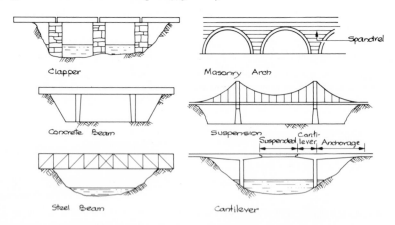

Fig. 25.1 Bridge types

25.1 Performance requirements
In order to provide the facility of safe crossing previously mentioned, the bridge must

a) be able to span between supports safely and economically and support the dead loading which will be applied in the form of traffic both in the immediate and in the reasonably foreseeable future;
b) provide sufficient clearance beneath to allow other forms of traffic to pass with reasonable freedom;
c) have stable supports so that no sinking at the ends of a span will take place;
d) be able to withstand the dynamic loading resulting from (i) vehicular movement across the span, (ii) water flow around the supports, (iii) wind pressures, since the structure may be in an exposed situation;
e) be durable since, once a bridge is provided, the population tend to rely on it because the alternatives are too costly in terms of time, money, or inconvenience;
f) be large enough to cater for the anticipated volume of traffic — a large number of traffic hold-ups result from bridges, many of them built before the twentieth century, being incapable of carrying the volume of present traffic;
g) have a pleasing appearance so as to blend with its surroundings and not become an eyesore;

h) be protected from degradation as a result of weather or the wear and tear of the traffic using it.
   Further requirements include
j) ease of maintenance – the Forth railway bridge with its continuous painting programme is a poor example of meeting this requirement;
k) accommodation of services – Having provided the means of bridging an obstacle, it is sound economics to make full use of the facility;
l) the ability to flex and take up small movement – the longer spans will need to be able to expand and contract as well as to flex as a result of the changing loading conditions;
m) the provision of safety features such as lighting, barriers, rain-water drainage, etc.

25.2 Components (fig. 25.2)

Abutment	The side support at the banks providing a resistance to both horizontal and vertical forces imposed on a bridge. Stability is achieved by self weight or ground anchors.
Anchor(age)	Heavy-mass concrete block used to anchor suspension cables or cantilever arms.
Arch	Vertical curved beam used to carry heavy loads across supports.
Bearing	Support between the deck and pier or abutment which carries the weight of the bridge.
Bolster	See 'Bearing'.
Catenary	The curve which a uniformly loaded cable takes up when hung between two points, e.g. on a suspension bridge.
Deck	That part of the bridge which carries the traffic loads and spreads them to the main structural supports.
Ground anchor	Anchorage for surface structures provided by drilling holes into the ground, inserting rods or cables, and grouting them in.
Piers	Intermediate supports between abutments, founded on firm ground.

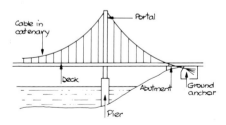

Fig. 25.2 Structural components

193

Portals	Towers providing high-level support to suspension cables.
Truss	Framework supporting bridge loads above the deck level.
Wing walls	Side walls which retain an embankment.

25.3 Bridge construction

The methods of bridge construction vary from site to site and contractor to contractor. They are also dictated by many factors which include the size of the spans; the materials to be used; the restrictions imposed by the location of the site, its topography, and access limitations; the structural design principles; and usage of the area over which the bridge spans.

However, whatever methods are used, they may be broken down into six distinct sections:

a) founding the piers and abutments;
b) construction of those piers, abutments, and portals;
c) provision of the structural span;
d) construction of the deck;
e) provision of the wearing surface;
f) incorporation of safety features and services.

An example of constructing a simple flat slab bridge carrying a minor road over a stream will serve to illustrate the problems and construction principles involved.

a) *The founding of the abutments* will depend on the nature of the strata, both of the banks of the stream and of the stream bed. The construction of the abutment will be affected by the velocity of the water flow, its change in level resulting from weather conditions, and the effects of scour action around any temporary works.

In order to provide a dry area in which to construct the foundation, interlocking sheet-steel piles could be driven around the foundation area from the bank on one side of the stream, to a depth suitable to prevent water entry. The foundations may then be excavated and constructed in dry working conditions.

b) *The abutment* must not only support the bridge but must also act as a retaining wall to prevent the carriageway falling into the stream. This prevention must be not only along the line of the road but also at right angles to it, which may require the extension of the abutment for widths greater than those required for the carriageway construction, or the use of wing walls.

The abutments may be constructed of stone, brick, or, more usually, in-situ reinforced concrete (fig. 25.3). In the latter case the interlocking sheet piles could be used as permanent shuttering, thus saving costs and at the same time protecting the concrete below the level of the stream from various harmful effects such as scour, erosion, and sulphate attack. A facing of other material may be applied to the concrete abutment in order to improve the appearance, while at the rear a protective coating of

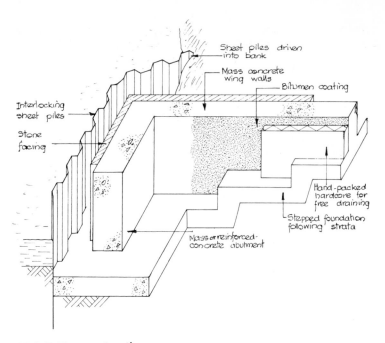

Fig. 25.3 Bridge construction

bituminous paint is applied to the vertical face and a land-drainage system is incorporated in order to reduce the horizontal thrusts due to wet back-fill material against the retaining wall (see Volume 3, Chapter 7).

c) In the case of small-span bridges, *the structural span* consists of precast, prestressed, concrete beams having various cross-sectional shapes. These beams are brought to the site by road and are lifted into position by a mobile crane. The tops of the abutments are rebated to form the bearing for the beams to seat on (fig. 25.4). Depending on the method of structural design, the bearing may incorporate facilities for movement, thus allowing for expansion, contraction, creep, and flexure.

d) *The deck* (fig. 25.5) generally comprises an in-situ reinforced-concrete topping to the precast beams. This topping provides the base for the carriageway construction as well as linking the beams into an integral unit, housing the various services (in ducts for ease of repair, maintenance, etc.), and providing anchorage for guard rails, barriers, lamp posts, and traffic signs.

The deck is cast in a similar manner to the concrete slabs described in Chapters 5 and 12. Alternatively, a rigid construction may be achieved by casting the beams and deck in-situ and linking them as an integral unit with the abutment. This in-situ work can provide additional construction problems in providing the soffit formwork with adequate support over the stream bed.

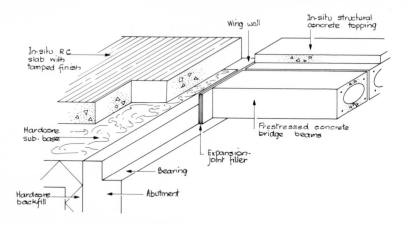

Fig. 25.4 Bridge bearing

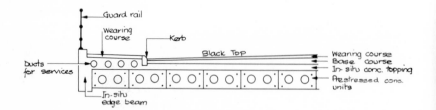

Fig. 25.5 Bridge deck

e) *The wearing surfaces* to both the carriageway and the footway are constructed in a similar manner to those detailed in Chapter 23. Provision for surface water may be either to a sewer or, in appropriate cases, a direct discharge into the stream below.

Where movement joints are incorporated into the structure there must be a similar facility in the wearing surface. This is provided by means of specially designed steel shoes which keep the two wearing surfaces apart while at the same time preventing the entry of dirt and water into the main structure.

f) *The erection of the overground equipment* has already been described in Chapter 24.

While only one basic form of bridge construction has been outlined, the problems associated with any simple bridge construction can be appreciated and their solution resolved for a given set of circumstances.

196

Index

tie, 58, 73
tiles, wall, 134
   background, 136
   fixing, 137
   materials, 134
   movement joint, 139
   shape, 135
tilt fillet, 81
timbering, 29, 36
   close, 30
   open, 30
toothed-plate connector, 82
Town and Country Planning Act, 7
traffic signs, 186
traps, 163
Tree Preservation Order, 7
tremie, 62
trench sheet, 29
truss, 77, 82, 194
trussed rafter, 82

undercoat, 144

valley, 78, 83
valves, 153
vapour barrier, 92, 96

vehicle, 142
verge, 78, 94, 97

waling, 30
wall-plate, 78, 87
waste appliances, 162
water, 20
   bar, 122
   closet, 157
   concreting, 48
   pipe, identification, 23
   supply systems, 148
   table, 28
water: cement ratio, 52
wearing surface, 196
weathering, 68, 70
welt, 99
wet edge, 144
windows, 101
   glazing, 103
   installation, 102
   schedule, 101
wing wall, 194

yoke, 58